You're Worth It!

But Do You Believe It?

Brent D. Earles

BAKER BOOK HOUSE
Grand Rapids, Michigan 49506

ISBN: 0-8010-3427-2

Printed in the United States of America

With deep respect for my dear friend,
Dick Meier, for having such a
profound effect upon my life, and
for making good sense in explaining true
self-worth to me when I needed to hear

Contents

Introduction

Something is really bothering me, and I want to get it off my chest right here at the very beginning. I want to know why somebody didn't give me a book like this when I was a teenager. Because if I could back up and be a teenager again, knowing what I know now, things would be much less traumatic—I think. Then again, some tough experiences are unavoidable. It's just part of growing up and becoming mature.

That still doesn't erase what I went through. If producers ever decide to make a movie about my adolescent years, it will have to be a horror flick. I can see the title now—I *Was A Teenage Paranoid.*

It started when my voice went haywire. Like some sort of weird TV blooper, it didn't match my face or my body. It was high one day, low the next. I began to be nervous. Then hair grew—in the strangest places! Don't laugh! At first, there were only a few hairs—peach fuzz—on my chin, under my arms, on my arms, on my legs, and in other places, too! I felt pretty stupid trying to figure out why this hair was popping up all of a sudden. I got more nervous.

Just about then one of the worst experiences happened. I started stinking! Yeah, you heard me right—B.O.! How was I supposed to know what deodorant was for? For all I knew, people rubbed it under their arms to make the hair grow there, and somehow I had accidentally gotten some of the stuff all over me! Suddenly I found out I had to put on that junk every day, or else I'd stink up the place. I was beginning to have my doubts about growing up. I yearned for the simple days of childhood, when I could run all day in the hot summer sun and sweat like crazy without stinking. Because a little kid's sweat hardly smells at all. Those days were over for good. The doors of a new world opened to me—the world of sticks, roll-ons, sprays, and extra-dry. I became even more nervous.

Who thought up the idea of teenagers' zits? I'm going to write a letter to my congressman when I find out. Because I was having a tough enough time as it was, without having bumps full of ooze on my face. Every time somebody looked at me I was afraid to talk—thanks to my squeaky voice. But I wondered if I was going to hear another crack about my "peach fuzz." I had to smell my underarms to make sure I wasn't stinking. And I had to guess which one of my zits the spectator thought to be the grossest.

Next came relationships. That's what really sent me over the edge. Here I was trying to hold everything together in a body bent on metamorphosis, when all kinds of pressures came—pressures to be a jock, to be a clown, to get drunk, to get high, to drive fast, to stay out late, to skip classes, to fall in love, to make love, to act wild, to rebel, to make high grades, to be an honor student, to turn in homework on time, to fit in, to go to church or not to go to church, to dress a certain way and be like one crowd, to dress an altogether different way and be like another crowd. Some days I felt like resigning from the human race. The good news is that my nervousness went away. The bad news is that I became paranoid.

Do you know what I battled the most? Myself. I was changing so fast I couldn't keep up with myself. The thing I changed the most was my mind. I was unsure about what I believed or what I knew. But I thought I was sure, and I sure acted sure. One thing I know now is that I was very unsure—of myself. I doubted myself. Sometimes I hated myself. I criticized myself. I worried a lot about what other people thought of me. Another thing I know now is that I wasn't paranoid. No, I was normal. What I went through is similar to what most teenagers go through. Especially that part about self-doubt.

Now you know why I'm writing this. Too many times I felt worthless. Most of the time it was simply because being a teenager is not the easiest thing in the world to be. So this is for everybody who is going through, or is about to go through, the secret traumas of growing up.

Don't hold back. Read it all—every single word. You're worth it!

1

Are You Your Friend?

My sister loves Ziggy—that chubby cartoon guy who can't do anything right. She is such a fanatic over him that I started reading his adventures on the comic pages. Sometimes ol' Ziggy really gets blue and down on himself. In one recent strip he said, "Every day in every way I'm getting better and better... at kidding myself."

How about you? How do you feel about yourself? Do you like yourself? If so, what do you like about yourself? If not, what do you dislike? Is it okay to like yourself? Or is it a sin? Is it more godly to think you're rotten, or to think you're valuable? Is a title like *You're Worth It!* too proud-sounding for a Christian book? And, finally, what do you think you're worth?

Sounds like a pop quiz, huh? But they are still good questions to think about. I hope you will. Because there exists

11

this ignorant idea that people are never supposed to feel good about themselves—that's so-called pride, arrogance, and conceit. Let me make one thing crystal-clear: God is very much against pride, and we're going to look at that in a later chapter through a different microscope. But it is possible to like yourself—as a person—as part of God's creation—without turning into a cocky, stuck-up brat.

Some people, though, are their own worst enemy, as the saying goes. Instead of getting better, they get worse. On the inside, a personal hate club is constantly at work in the mind, sending messages of self-defeat. Those little letters of hate mail say things like:

I'm no good.

I'm ugly.

I'm too fat.

I'm too skinny.

My ears are big.

I mess up everything.

I hate myself.

My friends don't even like me.

I'm dumb.

I don't have any talents.

I'm clumsy.

My nose is long.

My hair is too straight (or too kinky).

No wonder nobody likes me.

I won't get any dates.

I will never be any good.

Nobody is going to make me believe that people who feel this way about themselves have found the secret to humility and godliness. People who really feel this way have a warped understanding of themselves. If that's the way God wants people to feel about themselves, then why on earth did he go to the trouble of creating us?

Stop playing the I-hate-myself game. It's dangerous, because the longer you play it, the more you believe the messages you keep repeating. Pretty soon you'll act out how you feel about yourself. Don't believe me? Then why are teenagers—the age group battling most with inner feelings about self—the ones who are most often casualties of self-destruction?

In one of the classic movies of all time and one of his finest performances as an actor, James Dean portrayed the life of a teenager drowning in a tide of self-doubt and self-hate. The movie was called *Rebel Without a Cause*. That young man and many of his friends were so full of negative feelings about themselves, and they were so dejected on the inside, that they didn't have enough self-respect to keep themselves from destroying their young lives. Sad story, but a great message.

So many young people are trapped into acting out some prodigal-son script, and with no real cause. Except the one that burns down on the inside. The one that has made them believe they are worthless anyway, "so who cares what happens to me—who cares how bad off I get." Others go through the secret torture of self-rejection every day, but cover it with plastic smiles. Neither type sounds too happy.

God has a better plan. He wants you to look upon yourself as his unique creation. And through his Son Jesus, he wants to handcraft you day by day into one of his masterpieces. But not only *you*. He will help anyone who will come to him. Even though man is biased and accepts people on the grounds of how "special" they seem, God isn't like that. He accepts you as you are and works from there. The best news of all is that he never rejects anyone who calls out for him. But don't just call for his help, call for him!

God wants you to become a friend to yourself—certainly not your own worst enemy! Tear up all that hate mail piled around in your mind. Discard the old feelings of gloom and pessimism. Throw away the mind-cassette that ends by saying, "This person will self-destruct in thirty seconds." Make a pact with yourself today to work with yourself, not against yourself.

One reminder—and only a reminder because, as I promised, we will discuss it more later—proud braggarts are not helping themselves a bit. Egomania soon becomes lonelymania. Braggers might like themselves, but nobody else does. Besides, you know what? Most boasters boast to cover up for the worthless feelings they really have.

Today you have a chance to make a new friend.

Yourself.

In His Image:

> But he said to me,"My grace is sufficient for you, for my power is made perfect in weakness." Therefore I will boast all the more gladly about my weaknesses, so that Christ's power may rest on me (2 Cor. 12:9).

You're Worth it!

Challenge yourself with one of these projects and prove it:

1. Talk to one or both of your parents about what being a teenager was like for them.
2. Memorize 2 Corinthians 12:9.
3. Write down five qualities you would like to have, then choose one to work on this week.

2

Your *Sin*-drome

This syndrome, that syndrome. I get the idea from what I read and hear that everybody's got something wrong with him or her. Since a syndrome is "a group of signs and symptoms of abnormality," who knows—maybe all people do have something wrong with them. There usually is something a little "abnormal" about everyone.

As a matter of fact, to be abnormal today is the normal thing to do—the weirder, the better. Fads and crazes have always been a popular cover-up for the fear of being natural. They make a dandy little wall we put up around ourselves to keep from getting rejected and hurt. Nobody wants to be called strange. Remedy: Make being strange normal—make everything normal!

One problem. All our syndromes flow out of our *sin*-drome. Sin—that's the culprit. Our feelings of fear, self-consciousness, worry, paranoia, shyness, loudness, and dozens more, come from this enemy within.

Today's society tells us, "All people are basically good." But here's a shocker—people are not basically good! True, God has placed in each person's heart the basic desire to be good. Still, people are basically bad.

That sounds negative, I know. It sounds as if I'm saying everybody is cruel, unkind, and hateful. They're not, at least not on the outside. At heart, though, lives are twisted, crooked, and bent by selfishness, which is at the center of our *sin*-drome. Here's the odd thing. The more a person listens to that selfishness, the more self-centered he or she becomes. And the more self-centered you become, the more abnormal you feel. Catering to self only causes greater tension. How's that for a first-rate syndrome?

The truth is that nobody's "normal." Not in the sense that nothing is wrong with us. Confusing? Don't let it be. What I mean is that we all have unusual quirks and mannerisms. We all have our own personal hang-ups and imperfections— the things that make us different from other people.

That doesn't mean there isn't room for improvement. There always is. It just means that all the improvements in the world can't solve the real problem. Trying to clean up our act on the outside will not change anything on the inside.

Before you can get a long-lasting grip on feeling better about yourself, you need inside-out changes. That means forgiveness. That's the only way to solve the *sin*-drome. And sin is the greatest threat to becoming the best *you*.

Sin is like Mr. Hyde to Dr. Jekyll. Once it gets loose it warps a person. It makes a person abnormal. This is especially true of someone who has received Jesus Christ and his forgiveness. When a Christian slides back to the old ways of sin, it's like having a split personality—two people in one body. One part of the person wants to do right, the other part wants to do wrong. That's a *sin*-drome and a half.

Being constantly defeated by sin can be crushing to building self-confidence. Why? Because giving in to temptation is like failure, which is seldom a boost to the ego. Even while we put on a good front—trying to act normal to everyone who watches—in private the conscience stings us with jabbing reminders. This is one of the devil's wind-up toys meant to tear us down. Sometimes it is almost as if he whispers, "See how bad you are? You're not a very good Christian, are you? How could God love you? You can't even resist a tiny temptation." This clever mockery of his can be quite effective in making us feel rotten about ourselves. It's the ultimate *sin*-drome.

There is some good news, though. The conscience was designed by God for a reason. It's a warning buzzer. When it goes off, it signals the need for forgiveness. If we obey the signal and seek forgiveness, we can ward off the agony of feeling dominated by failure. Forgiveness gives us new power to be a better person, because it means God is with us. That doesn't make us perfect, but it does make us stronger. It makes us more normal, too, because nothing deforms a person like sin. It's the biggest ugly stick of all time. A lot of people show symptoms of having been clobbered by it. They have a *sin*-drome, if you know what I mean.

In His Image:

> *Therefore do not let sin reign in your mortal body so that you obey its evil desires.... For sin shall not be your master ...* (Rom. 6:12, 14).

You're Worth It!

Help yourself believe you are by trying one of the following morale-builders:

17

1. Ask God to help you have the strength to overcome the temptation that bothers you most.
2. Ask for God's forgiveness if some sin is tearing you down.
3. Try relaxing and being yourself—no walls, no faking, no masks—especially with your friends.

3

Temporary Amnesia

Supposedly, whenever a person gets conked extremely hard on the head, it can cause temporary amnesia. That means a person's memory is somehow blanked out for a short period of time. Any personal facts (name, address, age, and so on) are completely forgotten. Actually, this happens very rarely, or so I hear.

But one thing I know is that lots of teenagers suffer from some of these symptoms. They appear to be having a real identity crises. Self-discovery can be a spooky adventure, because there may be things about ourselves that we don't like. Not just physical features, either. There are deeper and more unpleasant things to face, such as being lazy, bad-tempered, too blabber-mouthed, overly shy, extra-jealous, and rebellious. You see, everybody has a secret reflection he or she doesn't like seeing in the mirror.

There are other things about self-discovery that make it difficult. For instance, the riddles. Those with teenage amnesia wonder, "Who am I? How should I act? Why do I do the things I do? What am I meant to be? Am I really being myself, or am I play-acting? What does it mean to *be myself*? Why do I feel like one person one day, and then like an altogether different person the next? Is it all right for me to have my own opinions? How can I form good opinions? Am I weird if I haven't made up my mind yet? Am I strange if I feel as if I'm losing my mind?"

What brings on all this confusion? Growing up. Yep, that's it. Here's what I mean. You're in a constant state of change. Actually, you always have been, but as a child you didn't realize it. Now you do. But at times you are changing so fast that even you can't keep up with it. The problem is that there are so many stages of maturity, and you are moving through them so quickly, that in just a short period of time you become almost a different person—more mature.

Battling that mature adult is the child in you. It seems as if your two selves have waged war against each other. Sometimes you find yourself being serious-minded. Then, before you know it, you are longing for old playthings even though you've outgrown them. You keep bouncing back and forth between acting like a grown-up and being a kid. The truth is, you are trying to find yourself. You know, like an amnesiac does.

Does that mean the adult must finally kill the child in you? No! Good grief, no! Unfortunately, this happens to some people. They turn out to be ultrasophisticates—the jaded, "but of course" elite. Their lives are always a dull moment. On the other hand, some people never grow up. They never learn to handle responsibility and never overcome their childishness.

The child in you should never die. But it must not prevent you from maturing, either. Gradually, those two sides of you should blend and become one. When that happens, your identity crisis will end. You will become a juvenile adult.

Did I make it sound easy? I didn't mean to, because it is a horrible struggle some days. There will be other days, though, when you feel as though you've mastered yourself. You will feel in control of your emotions. It will seem as if everything you say has flair and that all your actions are flawless. And then, just as soon as your self-consciousness begins to ebb away, a huge tidal wave of childhood will crash ashore. Bingo! The whack on your head sends you back into temporary amnesia.

Isn't growing up fun?

In His Image:

> He called a little child and had him stand among them. And he said: "I tell you the truth, unless you change and become like little children, you will never enter the kingdom of heaven. Therefore, whoever humbles himself like this child is the greatest in the kingdom of heaven" (Matt. 18:2–4).

You're Worth It!

Find out how much by doing one of the following:

1. Write a paragraph about the hardest thing to give up from your childhood.
2. Write a paragraph about what scares you most about becoming an adult.
3. Think about an adult you want to be like after your teenage years are over. Why do you want to be like him or her? What qualities do you admire in that person?

4

Impersonate Yourself

Comedians who do impersonations can be fun to watch. Almost all of them do famous personalities like John Wayne, Humphrey Bogart, Clark Gable, and the notorious Richard Nixon. A fellow by the name of Rich Little is known as one of the great impersonators. He can imitate not only speech styles but mannerisms and facial expressions. If you've ever seen him, you know what I'm talking about.

So what's my point? This: Less popular or barely noticed teenagers often fool themselves into thinking that if they act like somebody who is popular, then they too will become popular. They don't imitate classmates for comedy, but in a desperate search for attention.

It all begins quite innocently. Some jock, cheerleader, genius, or whatever is surrounded by friends and the choicest opposite-sex selections. Sparked by a tinge of envy, the ordinary people begin mental jumping jacks—"How can I become popular?" goes through their heads.

First comes style copying—dress like the studs or get a hair style like the gorgeous blonde who gets all the looks. Then stand like them. Sit like them. Walk like them. Laugh like them. A lot of this is more of a desperate reaction than it is an intentional plan.

Next come the more drastic measures. Participate in the same things the heroes do. Try to outclass them. Become best friends with them, if possible. But not for friendship's sake so much as for the hope of popularity. It happens, right? Oh, the games people play! Soon we have a clone, someone who walks, talks, sits, looks, acts, and believes like another person.

This creates quite a problem. For one, when the original person (the one being copied) changes a bit, then his or her impersonator has to change, too. Before long, the person being imitated figures everything out and takes the upper hand in the relationship. The copycat becomes a puppet on a string.

A bigger problem exists, though. An individual has been lost. Exactly right—the imitator. The uniqueness of that person has been plastic-coated with the image of another person. And as long as that's so, the things that God made special in that person are lost—the laugh, the smile, the emotions, the style, the whole person. I think that's sad. So does God.

There is no substitute for being yourself. Develop your own style. Be your own trend-setter. Choose your own dreams. Create your own image. Enjoy the company of your own friends, no matter how many nor how few, for they accept you the way you are and stand behind you as you grow into an even better person. Dress in the superb excellence of your own imagination and budget! Express your own well-thought-out ideas. And, above all, don't compromise the beliefs that you truly hold dear.

Now this is not an invitation to become a mustang or renegade. The punk trends of our day are supposed to be an objection to anything normal or predictable. But even though the "punkers" are quite abnormal by ordinary standards, they're still predictable. In their attempt to be different from everyone else, they are all alike—equally weird!

What I'm trying to say is, "Impersonate yourself." The more you learn about life—what you like and dislike, what you want to stand for, what you want to be like, what you want to accomplish, what you care about, what you enjoy doing—let that sink down into you. Let it become a part of you. Then radiate it. Allow the things that are you to shine out of you.

You might never become popular in school. But at least you will be your own person. No, you might not grow up to become a John Wayne, a Barbara Walters, or whomever you think is worth imitating. But impersonating yourself is a lifelong challenge, and it sure beats living in the shadows of other people.

In His Image:

Dear friend, do not imitate what is evil but what is good.—(3 John 11).

You're Worth It!

Here's your chance at specializing in individuality:

1. Write down some of the qualities you hope to develop in becoming the you God wants you to be.
2. Name some of the standards you won't compromise for the sake of recognition.
3. Think of a couple things you can do as well as or better than anyone else your age.
4. Earn or save enough money to buy a new article of clothing that expresses the classic style you like. (Be sure your parents approve.)

5

Nobody's a Nobody

One day a guy who had battled his inferiority complex by himself for as long as he could went to see a psychiatrist. The doctor sat in his plush leather chair, and the patient lay down on the contoured couch. With pen and pad in hand the psychiatrist listened to his patient talk.

"Doc, my problem is that I feel inferior to everyone else. I don't know why, but somehow I've convinced myself that I'm just not good at anything," the distraught man began.

"I see," the psychiatrist answered as he jotted down some notes.

"Can you help me, Doc? Can you tell me what's wrong with me?" The man was at his wits' end.

"I will certainly try," the doctor replied, "but it is liable to take us more than one session."

The man agreed and so began to see the psychiatrist

every week. After several weeks and several hundred dollars in charges, the doctor announced they were nearing the end.

Feeling quite relieved that an answer to his misery had been found, the man asked, "Well, Doc, what did you find?"

The psychiatrist answered, "After many hours of careful study of my notes of everything you've told me, I have come to the conclusion that you *are* inferior!"

Had you going there for a minute, didn't I? Even though this is only a cute joke, there are people who feel just like that man did. People who feel inferior are people who think they are incompetent and inadequate.

How can you tell if somebody has got an inferiority complex? Watch for these signs. A person who feels inferior will repeat them often:

1. Attention-getting shenanigans. The person will continually goof off in class or cause trouble to get attention.
2. Extreme shyness. The individual will avoid social activities and be as reclusive as a brown spider in winter.
3. Perfectionism. Even an above-average performance irritates this person. It's got to be perfect or else it is rotten. Trouble is, there's no such thing as "perfect."
4. Possessiveness. He or she will cling to one or two people for security. Usually those friends have lesser abilities, and the person with the complex will try to dominate them.
5. Criticism. The person who feels inferior tries to build himself or herself up by tearing others down.
6. Supersensitivity. At the same time, this person cannot bear the tiniest criticism and will run to defensiveness in order to avoid any comparison with failure.
7. Enviousness. The individual ignores his or her own personal qualities and centers on the strengths of

other people. Envy and jealousy surge in and control the emotions.

8. Hyper-embarrassment. A person battling feelings of inferiority is easily upset by the teasing of others.

If you read the signs and said, "Oh, no, that's me!" join the club. Most people feel incompetent and inadequate from time to time. Some of these feelings are normal. But if you're plagued by all eight of these things every day, then you probably feel like the guy in the story at the beginning of this chapter.

Everybody needs to know that nobody's a nobody. Every person has God-given worth. It's like somebody once said: "God don't make no junk!" He certainly doesn't make "junk people." Write this down and tack it on the wall—GOD STANDS BY HIS PRODUCT.

But here's what happens sometimes—the product doubts itself. Have you ever done that? Gone into deep self-doubt? Bad trip. All the gears get stripped, and the person is permanently jammed into neutral. That takes you nowhere real fast.

Of course, it's silly to pretend that one chapter, or even this book, is going to cure any feelings of inferiority you might have. There's no such thing as waving a wand to bring a miracle cure. But one thing I'm sure of, if you will start concentrating on yourself as God's deliberate creation and stop focusing on all the mistakes you make, is that a special peace will begin to take over your heart. It's a peace that is so wonderful no one can find words to describe it!

Soon you will be saying, "Hey! I'm not a nobody after all!"

In His Image:

Do not be anxious about anything, but in everything, by prayer and petition, with thanksgiving, present your requests to God. And the peace of God, which transcends all understanding, will guard your hearts and your minds in Christ Jesus (Phil. 4:6–7).

You're Worth It!

It's your turn to help build a positive self-image. Choose one:

1. Pick out the signs of feeling inferior (see p. 26–7) that plague you most, then pray for God to to help you get over them. (Clue to victory: you might have to pray more than once.)
2. Spend some time alone with one of your parents. Play a game, go shopping, or just talk.
3. Make a gift for someone for no special occasion, but just to give of yourself to someone else.

6

What Makes You, You?

Simple. Personality—that's what makes you an original. God painted your portrait with colorful brush marks. He painted your environment and your family. He etched in some other influences and your abilities. After that, with a few subtle brushstrokes he crafted your potential. Then, after the basic scheme of your life was designed, he breathed life into you. Suddenly, you were a squalling brat! But you were no surprise to God.

In some cases, because of sin, you were not always touched by the right influences or best environment. That was not God's design, but it was not his fault, either. Still, your world was making an imprint on your life, so that today you are pretty much a result of your inheritance and upbringing. Overriding all this is the blueprint God has for you. Through Jesus Christ you can undergo a radical personality improvement. At last! God signs his name in the corner of your canvas.

Now what? Is that the end? Just accept Jesus as your Savior and Shazam! all is well? Not exactly that easy. You see, developing your personality is a daily adventure. You will find it very much like most adventures—frightening, challenging, fun, boring, rewarding, and disappointing.

Here's the thing. You've already got a basic personality to work with. You may or may not like it, but it's what you will have to accept and build on. Some people never reach their potential because they refuse to put forth any effort to improve themselves. They just mope around and moan about how they wish they had a better personality.

Below you will find a sketchy chart of personality strengths and weaknesses. Look it over. You will have some of each. I'm including this to let you know that God is in the business of turning weaknesses into strengths. God does not demolish your basic personality when you come to Christ and then start again. He just reshapes you. Where once you were weak and flawed, he makes you strong and distinct—if you work with him.

Weaknesses	Strengths
weak-willed/defeated	strong willed/determined
self-centered	self-sacrificing
stingy	generous
bad-tempered	easy-going
undependable	productive
revengeful	forgiving
fearful	confident
unemotional	warm
loud	friendly
negative	optimistic

uninvolved	enthusiastic
inconsiderate	sensitive
pushy	personable
stubborn	flexible
unmotivated	determined
sharp-tongued	humorous

Wouldn't it be nice if we could all be a hodgepodge of the strengths, instead of being a mixture of strengths and weaknesses? Forget it. It's not going to happen in this lifetime. But it's worth working at.

Mark your weaknesses, then look across to the strengths in the other list. That's what God wants to build into your personality—at least a bit anyway—to help you fulfill your potential. Mark your strengths, too. Look at their opposites and you will see what happens when you push your personality overboard, or what can happen to it if you suffer burnout. When you have marked both sides, you will have a kind of picture of yourself the way others see you. These are the traits of your personality that make you, *you*.

Don't get mad about your weaknesses. And don't be proud of your strengths. There's plenty to work on. By the way, although you will meet people who have a similar personality to yours (and you probably won't get along too well), that doesn't mean you will be exactly alike. In fact, you will learn that even though people have matching personalities, they are still very different.

Why? Because God makes people the same way he makes snowflakes—if you know what I mean.

In His Image:

That is why, for Christ's sake, I delight in weaknesses, in insults, in hardships, in persecutions, in difficulties. For when I am weak, then I am strong (2 Cor. 12:10).

31

You're Worth It!

Join in the fun of self-improvement and become even more valuable:

1. Share the lists of strengths and weaknesses in this chapter with your parents. See what they might have to say.
2. Choose a strength you're weak in to work on this week.
3. Think of a Bible character who had a lot of strengths and do a brief study of his or her life.

7

The Bashful Blues

How about shyness? And now that the subject has come up, what about introverts? Is there any hope for the quiet types? Does everyone have to be a crowd-pleaser to make it in life? Is shyness bad? Is being introverted worse than being outgoing?

This is touchy stuff. You know why? Because several of the people reading this right now grapple with shyness. Meeting people and making friends is tough for them. Maybe that's you. It isn't so unusual. Lots of teenagers in this world have been branded with the "shy" or "quiet" label. If you are one of them, this news on the bashful blues might be just the ticket for you.

First we need to make one thing clear. There is a mammoth difference between being socially shy and fearfully withdrawn. Remember our little chat about the inferiority complex a couple of chapters ago? Well, yank me down if I'm getting on my soap box, but *extreme* shyness points to self-defeat. If a person is running away from relationships altogether, that just doesn't size up. And being introverted or extroverted hasn't got a hoot to do with it.

I'm not talking about the ordinary shyness most everybody feels at one time or another, but about what I call the Lone Ranger syndrome. Here's a guy rushing in and out of a situation, wanting to be a hero, but afraid to reveal his true identity. Result: withdraw and avoid being vulnerable, because being vulnerable means taking a risk with your heart. Somebody might hang you out to dry. That hurts.

You don't need a degree in psychology to figure out that nobody wants to get hurt. Likewise, just a pinch of common sense reveals that withdrawal isn't a constructive way to cope with fear. In fact, since these types often find that adulthood doesn't offer much escape, they frequently become the loneliest, most depressed people in the world.

Being shy is a whole different problem with its own pitfalls. For instance, shy people are often called "stuck-up" or "snobbish." Right? Ever had that happen to you? By simply being quiet and reserved, you get labeled with a tag: "He thinks he's better than the rest of us." Girls, of course, are equally prone to such attacks.

Here's another myth about shy people—they aren't very smart. Because a person is quieter than others, it is sometimes assumed that he or she isn't thinking very hard. Is that dumb, or what? It's usually the opposite. The shy person is full of ideas, but afraid to express them.

That brings us to the nitty-gritty. What are shy people afraid of? After all, at last check, you don't get beaten up or killed for trying to be friendly, or for trying to give your viewpoint. So what is causing the fear? Two things:

1. *Rejection*. I hate being laughed at, don't you? Few things

hurt more than being turned away by someone you trusted enough to tell your feelings. The embarrassment of it all just doesn't seem worth it. To be sure, those extroverts appear to have it all together. But can I let you in on a secret? They don't, but they cover their fears by being bubbly. Aren't people crazy? We're all afraid of the same things, but instead of giving each other breathing room, we put on more pressure by hiding behind our masks. Here's a hint: If you learn to accept others as they are, and yourself as you are, then opening up will slowly become easier.

2. *Failure*. This is sort of related to the first one, because we figure a big blooper will surely land us in the rejection pile. So why take the chance? Shutting yourself up while shutting others out is no cure for failing. The way I see it, we all blow it if we're given plenty of opportunities. But the colossal foul-up of all is missing out on friendships and teenage fun. And that's what shyness will do—if you let it. Learn to laugh at yourself. It helps you to keep from taking your mistakes so seriously.

Bottom line. Not everybody is cut out to be the life of the party. That's okay. Parties need to have more than one person to keep them lively. Go ahead and be involved. The more you work at meeting people and talking to them, the sooner those bashful blues will become a melody of joy.

In His Image:

Two are better than one, because they have a good return for their work: If one falls down, his friend can help him up. But pity the man who falls and has no one to help him up! (Eccles. 4:9–10).

You're Worth It!

Put something of your own into these and you will get an even better "you" in return:

1. Strike up a conversation with a classmate you have never talked to before.
2. Name three reasons why people should like you.
3. Ask God once a day, all week long, to help you trust him to give you the inner confidence you need.

8

Anybody's Hostage

Do you remember the Iranian hostage crisis? Americans were held captive in Iran more than four hundred days. It was one of the most terrible events in our history. Can you imagine being kept under guard like that? They missed Christmas with their families. And we questioned their safety all along. No day was sweeter than the one when they came home—free!

I can tell by the look in your eye that you are starting to know me. You think I've been loading my gun. No, not me. Well, okay—so you caught me red-handed. But the good thing about my bullets is that when they strike the heart they bring life! Please believe me, I'm not trying to wound anybody.

Pressure—that's my point here. You know a few things about pressure don't you? The agony of having to come up to snuff, especially around the people your age. You've probably heard it called "peer pressure," but I've got a better name for it—"fear pressure." Like Dean Martin once said, "Show me a man who doesn't know the meaning of the word *fear*, and I'll show you a dummy who gets beat up a lot!" With teenagers, the "beating" is usually verbal torture or intimidation.

Fear pressure is a boiler room—either act, dress, and believe as "the group" does, or else cook! Being roasted is probably a more accurate description. Why all this pressure, anyway? Just for the sake of acceptance? Just to be "in"?

Don't get me wrong. I'm not saying you should isolate yourself from your age group. It would be silly to become a radical, refusing to be like other teenagers in any way. Whew! Isn't that a relief? God doesn't expect you to be bug-eyed, with slicked-down hair.

Absolute alikeness is what I'm voting against. It's the herd instinct, which accuses anyone slightly different of being a second-class citizen, that bugs me. All people should be free to be and become themselves. Having to conform to some set pattern to avoid ridicule is ridiculous. Don't fall for it. Start a new fad of your own by being yourself.

If you allow the herd to make your decisions, you will have to toe their mark. Soon you lose your self-expression entirely. In other words, you become a puppet or a robot. The longer this goes on, the more the handcuffs pinch. Eventually, you are a total hostage to the whims of your peers. What causes such a thing to happen? Fear of rejection. That's pressure in the first degree.

Let me illustrate how severe this pressure can be. Ruth W. Berenda did a study some time ago on the subject. She and a few co-workers brought ten teenagers into a classroom and told them they were going to be tested on how well they could see. In the test they held up cards with three lines drawn on each. The lines were labeled A, B, and C. Each line was an obviously different length from the other two. Some-times A was the longest line. Sometimes B was, and so on.

Anyway, the students were instructed to raise their hands when the person testing them pointed to the longest line. One catch. Nine of the students had been brought in ahead of time. They were coached to go along with the researchers' plan and vote for the *second* shortest line. They were really testing that lone unprepared subject. Would he or she have the courage to go against the group and vote for the line that was obviously the longest?

In they came. Right off the bat the nine raised their hands when the researcher pointed to the second shortest line. The lone guy frowned, looked at them, looked back at the lines, wagged his head a little, then raised his hand with the group. The testers repeated the instructions, "Raise your hand when we point to the longest line." Card after card, the one guinea pig would agree with the group that a short line is longer than a long line. And why? Fear pressure.

Here's the amazing thing—the researchers brought in many other teenagers, one at a time, to join that group of nine. And in more than 75 percent of the cases the un-coached teenagers went along with the group. Can you be-lieve that?

To me that's outrageous! Parrots are birds, right? Not people. Then again, maybe some people are parrots. Which would mean, of course, they stand the risk of being stuck in a cage. If it were me, I wouldn't want to be anybody's hostage.

So I'm thumbing my nose at fear pressure. How about you?

In His Image:

For none of us lives to himself alone and none of us dies to himself alone. If we live, we live to the Lord; and if we die, we die to the Lord. So, whether we live or die, we belong to the Lord (Rom. 14:7–8).

You're Worth It!

Be courageous enough to accept one of these challenges:

1. Name a time you went along with the group just to keep from getting laughed at.
2. Name some of the things you've been pressured to do, but had the courage to say no.
3. Ask your parents if they ever got into trouble by listening to the encouragement of the wrong crowd.

9

Square Pegs
in a Round World

In 1954 Jerry Lewis made a funny movie that had a neat message. The movie was called *The Delicate Delinquent*. The main character, Sidney, played by Lewis, was a wacky young man who longed to find a place where he could fit in. He wanted to belong—to be a part of somebody's group. His desperation led him to join up with a street gang that constantly caused trouble.

It didn't work. The kid was too sensitive and kind to hurt anything or anyone. So he kept feeling left out, until one day a cop tried to help him. The cop sort of took him on as a project, trying to get him to believe in himself. Sidney tried to act tough, but his bravest efforts ended up as clumsy mistakes. Each failure drove him deeper, but he finally came to trust the officer who was giving him spare time in the evenings.

Suddenly, Sidney came up with a brilliant idea—he decided to become a cop! See how badly he wanted to belong? His friend was reluctant, but promised at least to give him a test. A few nights later he brought over a box. He opened it and dumped out several geometrical blocks. Then he told Sidney he had one minute to put the blocks back into their correct slots. Of course, Lewis was hilarious. He kept jamming triangular blocks into square holes and square ones into round holes. He failed.

But that little scene had a message, which was the theme of the whole show—Sidney was a square peg in a round world. He didn't fit. I think it was a good message, because nearly everybody has felt that way. Sidney, in a way, is a reflection of us all. No matter how hard we try, there are times when it just doesn't seem as if we belong anywhere.

Maybe you have felt that way a time or two. Karen and Richard Carpenter sang a song for thousands who have. It was called "Rainy Days and Mondays." Some of the words went like this:

Talking to myself and feeling old
Sometimes I'd like to quit, nothing ever seems to fit
Hanging around, nothing to do but frown
Rainy days and Mondays always get me down
What I've got they used to call the blues
Nothing is really wrong, feeling like I don't belong
Walking around, some kind of lonely clown
Rainy days and Mondays always get me down

Sometimes it is more of a mood than it is a reality. We get to feeling down and can't figure out why. Moods are like that. They creep in and scare us into believing that we don't fit in anywhere.

And yet, in another sense, we *don't* belong. Hear me out. This world—its philosophies, wickedness, and emptiness—isn't our real home. The Bible teaches that we're pilgrims.

Sure, we live here and have a reason for being here. But we don't "belong" to the evil way of things. That makes us square pegs in a round world. If you don't agree, just live a godly life and see if worldly unbelievers don't take a few pot shots at you.

The truth is, if you try to please the Lord with your life, you won't fit in with many of the world's people. Not because you don't want to, but because you don't have common interests. That presents you with a gut-wrenching decision: Will you do right and face rejection, or will you go against your conscience and suffer the consequences? How do you like those apples?

Here's the good news—you still belong somewhere if you choose to do right. You can make friendships with other Christians, and you should. You still fit in with your family at home. I know you're growing up, but they need you there and you need them. You belong on this planet, too. That is, God has a plan for your life. Accomplish it, and you will find your place. In the meantime, to feel like you fit in, hang out with the people who love you, accept you, and encourage you to be the best God has in mind for you.

Oh, I almost forgot. Sidney, the delicate delinquent, finally became a cop. The square peg found a square hole.

In His Image:

> If you belonged to the world, it would love you as its own. As it is, you do not belong to the world, but I have chosen you out of the world . . . (John 15:19).

You're Worth It!

Build your feelings of belongingness by doing one of the following:

1. Talk to your parents individually and tell them you love them. Be serious and try not to giggle.

2. Thank one of your Christian friends for his or her friendship.
3. Find three Bible verses that teach that you belong to God's family.

10

Put-Downs

I've got a new way to quote an old cliché: "Sticks and stones may break my bones, but words are a lot more painful." Like everybody else, I went to Mom for advice when cruel remarks first came my direction. When she told me just to ignore them, it sounded pretty easy to do—until the next day. Naturally, the kids spouted off again. So I yanked one of them down and bashed his head against the merry-go-round. I was an innocent little second-grader at the time.

A few years later a similar incident came up. Being the mild-tempered guy that I was, I grabbed the smart-mouth who was badgering me and threw him up against the jungle gym. (I was a playground thug.) Then something happened that I hadn't expected. He promptly began mopping up the concrete with my face. It was bad news. Since that day, fist fights have failed to recapture my interest.

I can still remember that day, though. And I can recall

sitting in the principal's office, waiting for him to show up and add another insult to my insults and injuries. There I was, a fourth-grader, listening to the clock tick away the moments before justice prevailed. But on the inside I was thinking, "That guy had no right to say those things. He had no reason at all." So, you see, despite my beating and having to see the head honcho, the put-downs were still grinding their heels into my heart.

In high school I wasn't much of a fighter, but that didn't keep me from trying to get even for unkind teasing. I would snipe back, sometimes with downright cutting remarks. It's easy to be brutal with words, you know.

Let me clear up something. I didn't have it that rough, really! I ran pretty much with the "in" crowd. And I guess I was fairly popular. I stayed out of trouble, made good grades, and was very involved in my school's activities. "So what?" you say.

That wasn't meant to sound like bragging. I said all that to say this: even though I was "normal," I received my share of painful put-downs. Those barbs and arrows seem ridiculous now, but at the time they were deadly. Imagine what it was like for the ones who were unpopular.

Maybe you are under attack right now. It's almost like a war, isn't it? Every day somebody takes a shot at your looks, your character, your family, your beliefs, your clothes, or any number of a hundred other things. And most of their shots wound you. They cut into you, and it hurts deeply. You'd like to tell your parents, but it sounds so childish. If you tell them this silly stuff, they'll think you're immature. But the hurt won't go away.

Sometimes these put-downs come in the shape of jokes. In study hall, or between classes, a few people were just kidding around. Nobody really meant what was being said. It was just playful harassment. Everybody walked away acting normal, but most of them also walked away wondering if the teasing they received was for real. Do you know what I'm talking about?

This time of life for you is full of struggles. You are eager for freedom, acceptance, identity, romance, success, and so on, and being knocked down by sharp criticism makes all those things appear impossible. It's agonizing to have to hear constant verbal torture about being too tall, or skinny or fat, or red-headed, big-eared, long-nosed, freckled, oddly dressed, poor, clumsy, dumb, and who knows how many other things. Thank God for the days when nobody says an unkind word. Amen?

I wish I could offer some comfort. However, there is no blanket answer. You can—and should—cast your cares upon the Lord. Get the healing that only he can give. Still, the pain of those uninvited cruelties does not go away quickly. The only sure way to endure the put-downs is to have strong self-confidence built around Christ at the center of your life. Even then, you will receive your share of arrows.

No matter what the experts say, there are times when we would rather face sticks and stones instead of words.

In His Image:

> ... whoever spreads slander is a fool. When words are many, sin is not absent, but he who holds his tongue is wise. . . . The lips of the righteous know what is fitting, but the mouth of the wicked only what is perverse (Prov. 10:18–19, 32).

You're Worth It!

Heal old wounds by putting one of the following to work for you:

1. If someone has cut you down recently, ask God to forgive that person, and ask him to help you forgive the tongue-lasher, too.
2. If you have hurt someone with your words, ask for his or her forgiveness.
3. Meditate on the verbal attacks Jesus went through.

11

The Back Door to Greatness

Old Ben Franklin said some downright neat stuff, you know it? Here's one of my favorites: "The man who does things makes many mistakes, but he doesn't make the biggest mistake of all—doing nothing." Did you hear that? If you plan to improve yourself, you should expect to goof up now and then. Failing is one of the ingredients of success. It's the back door to greatness for those who never say die. Remember: *If at first you don't succeed, try, try again.*

Failure is at the root of teenage washout. Fear of failure is crippling. It stops a lonely person from meeting new people; it prevents a guy from asking out a cute girl who has caught his eye; it swallows up the excitement of participating in a school function; it makes cowards of students who want to get involved in classroom discussions; it sidetracks quitters from any challenge that is too big for a chicken to accept.

But how can failure do all that, and more, to ruin the hopes of teenagers—people with everything ahead of them? The clue is in self-esteem—by mangling your self-esteem. I haven't met a person yet who was interested in being a disgraceful laughingstock. Behind the word *failure* is the emotion of embarrassment. And you already know that embarrassment for a teenager is the next worst thing to death.

So why chance it, right? Why run the risk of falling flat on your face? Wouldn't it be much easier to drift through high school? To go unnoticed and thus unhurt by the flames of failure? To never have to know the pain of being a reject? To never have to pick yourself up, brush away the dirt, and wipe away the tears, only to try again and perhaps fail again?

Why risk the plunge? Because if you don't learn to launch out with dreams and ideas now, chances are you will be spellbound by the fear of failure long after your teenage years evaporate. But the teenager with guts enough to withstand failure eventually wins. And he or she is usually respected by a better breed of friend than the ones who kick a guy who's down.

Fear of failure isn't the real problem. It's lack of faith that needs to be smoked out. Faith has nothing to do with adventureless defeat. Faith is the vitamin you need for achievement. The question is: How much do you believe God can and will do in your life? The character of your faith is measured by what it takes to stop you. Some people are afraid of having faith, because they know if they start to believe—really believe—then they must try. And trying involves risk.

During these fast-moving teenage years an important trait is begging to be developed. It's the ability to dream big. Not pie-in-the-sky fantasizing, but a passion that believes with the whole heart that God wants to work miracles in and through your life. Begin to believe this and you will leave your fingerprints in your high school's memory books. What's more, you will be ready to test your faith when you reach the major leagues of life.

Remember though, self-esteem is a crucial part of whether or not you will combat failure head-on. If you are really down on yourself, chances are you won't have the gumption to get involved. With a horrible self-image, fear of failure will keep you from running for student council, from trying out for cheerleader, from playing solos in band or singing solos in choir, from trying out for the debate team or the school play, from lacing up the hightops and giving basketball a shot, from fighting for a spot on the newspaper or yearbook staff, and from being a fearless witness for Jesus Christ to your classmates who need a Savior.

But if you let your teenage years fly by, unfulfilled because you didn't try the challenges created just for you, then all you will have to cling to is regret. In fact, it's likely to become the story of your life.

In the words of John Greenleaf Whittier:

> For of all sad words of tongue or pen,
> The saddest are these: "It might have been!"

Don't make the biggest mistake of all. Don't do *nothing*!

In His Image:

For though a righteous man falls seven times, he rises again . . . (Prov. 24:16).

You're Worth It!

Are you ready to risk yourself?

1. Share your testimony of faith in Jesus Christ with an unsaved friend.

2. Join or try out some activity in your school that really interests you (provided your parents approve). Don't let fear of failure stop you.
3. Find a key verse of Scripture that helps you fight back when you feel like giving up. Then memorize it.

12

Is "Average" a Mediocre Word?

Have you noticed that some people just seem to have a special knack? It appears that there is nothing they can't do. Good grades come easily for them; popularity is like a second nature; they're athletic; they can sing; talent flows from their fingers in art and writing; and worst of all, they're all-around nice people. You'd like to find a reason to hate them, but you can't.

By comparison, the rest of us are garden-variety specimens. We're off the rack; they're tailor-made. Only on our very best days can we be what they are every day. Plainly said, we are common—average. This can be the source of disappointment and resentment. After a while we get fed up with being just another ordinary speck on the vast horizon of humanity. Being average can be hard to settle for, but for some it is an achievement. What are your feelings about "average"?

First of all, let me say that average doesn't necessarily mean mediocre. Falling short of potential is not what I'm talking about, since no one should settle for less than his or her best. It's crummy for a person to be third-rate when more ability aches to be used. But what about the person who pours everything into it and still comes out C+ by comparison to what a more gifted individual can do? A cold reality, huh?

If you don't mind, I'll toss out a couple of my ideas on the subject, and you can weigh them alongside your own. These are just opinions. And you know what they say: "Opinions are like noses—everybody's got one." Here are a couple of mine. When you get to the "You're Worth It!" section at the end of this chapter you can fire off yours.

1. I *think "average" people are taking a bum rap*. God gives everyone a specialty. Even those who are ordinary in many respects are gifted with some unique talent. They may not shine with superstardom in high school, but they quietly get the job done. One day, very unexpected by those peers who enjoyed teenage fame, that "average" person with a single forte grows up to be a master in the field of his or her knack. At many a ten-year high-school class reunion, jaws hang open in amazement at the success of the nobody who used to go around acting "medium."

Do you follow what I'm saying? Don't underestimate the people in your school who rarely get recognition. Those are the ones who grow up to be tomorrow's crackerjacks. And if you are down on yourself because you blend in with the common masses, keep giving your all. Be the best "average" person in your school. It is only by struggling that a butterfly escapes the cocoon.

2. I *think a lot of high school "heroes" are in for a big surprise*. Life won't always come on a silver platter. Later on, "heroes" have to learn how to adapt to struggling—something they hardly

knew in school. I've seen it happen. It was such a shock for some that they couldn't cope. They were so used to having it easy that adjusting to hard work was not in their chemistry.

At the same time, some people who were "average" in high school kept clipping along at their usual, regular pace. Nothing fancy, just steady-as-she-goes. It's like the old story of the race between the rabbit and the turtle. If you're a "rabbit," be advised that you can't depend upon your speed or ability to carry you through. It takes more than that to cross the finish line—much more! But if you're a "turtle," don't forget that you will have to stick out your neck to get anywhere. Clamming up in your shell is mediocrity in the worst way. Hiding behind your unadorned self is a copout. It's an excuse to duck the gut-wrenching work.

No matter what your abilities are, never get a stomach for business-as-usual. The one who settles for living in ruts—who laps up the muddy puddles of mediocrity—will never climb a mountaintop to taste the crystal-clear waters that sparkle with potential fulfillment.

To answer the question in the chapter title—no, "average" does not have to be a mediocre word. It just depends on the turtle.

In His Image:

> Do you not know that in a race all the runners run, but only one gets the prize? Run in such a way as to get the prize (1 Cor. 9:24).

You're Worth It!

Choose to participate in life in a more than mediocre way:

1. What are your opinions about those whose *best* efforts keep coming up "average"?
2. Ask your parents if any of their "average" classmates became specialists in a field no one expected.
3. Consider your strengths and then make a list of every different profession you could master by working at it.

13

Go for It!

Think of a color— any color, not necessarily your favorite. Whoa! Not so quickly! Take your time and let that color flood your mind. What color are you imagining? Red? Yellow? Blue? Aw, come on, you can do better than that. Try green!

Green?

Yes, green. No, not green as in dollar bills; not green as in "wet behind the ears"—immature green; not green as in "green with envy"; not green as in unripe fruit. I'm talking about green as in the traffic light. Better known as go-for-it green.

We've got too many red-thinkers. "Stop!" is their motto. It's impossible to get them going, so they never get anywhere.

There are about as many yellow-thinkers. They move at an

extremely slow pace because of excess caution. When they get somewhere it's about twenty years later than everyone else did. Their mental hang-ups are nearly as bad as the red-thinkers.

Blue-thinkers? Well, even though there is no such traffic light, some people motor through life with this frame of mind. They are gloomy, depressed, overcast people—blue! They wander around. Sometimes they go forward, but most of the time they look at the future through the rearview mirror. They're headed backward.

The basic snag for these three kinds of thinkers is an absence of self-confidence. Painted upon the flashing lights of red, yellow, and blue are five bold-face letters: I C-A-N'-T! I'm sorry to say that the ones who believe they can't usually make their predictions come true. As Henry Ford once said, "Think you can, think you can't; either way you'll be right."

Self-confidence might be an easy thing to talk about, but it isn't so easy to come up with. Right? You're probably thinking, "Really! I've got a hard enough time trying to remember my locker combination, coping with taking a shower with other people looking, and passing geometry. Besides, everybody knows teenagers don't have self-confidence. They're too busy acting casual to get messed up with psychology."

Okay, point well taken. But please hear me out. Because there are thousands of teenagers who face each day with about as much confidence as a matador fighting off a bull with a wet noodle. Oh, sure, plenty fake self-assurance real well with a smoke screen of cockiness. If the truth could be known, common panic runs red-hot in the veins of more than a few at your school.

God has a cure for that. And it isn't a cocky, conceited brand of confidence. Nor is it a one-time vaccination from the inner trembles; you'll have to keep refilling the prescription:

1. *Change the way you look at yourself.* Most of us are tempted to think that the answer to the mystery of self-confidence

lies simply within our human powers. Phooey! God's Word teaches that without Christ we are nothing—absolute zeros! But with him we are strengthened to do all things. Our confidence, then, does not rest with a strong self. Maybe we should change it from self-confidence to Christ-confidence.

2. *Get new mental pictures.* Permission is granted for positive daydreaming. Imagine yourself in difficult situations. Act them out in your mind, seeing yourself doing what is extra-ordinary and right. Fear wins out too often because a person can't imagine really succeeding. *Caution*: Don't get lost in your daydreams. Bring them to life!

3. *Set your expectations higher.* Turn up your achievement power-booster one notch from the last time. A person never reaches a mountaintop in one super-jump. It can be done only by climbing *one rock higher*, step by step. If you expect only a little from yourself, then "a little" is all you will get. And a little confidence is all you will have.

4. *Try harder.* Nothing builds Christ-confidence like suc-cess—and nothing brings success like a second effort or even a third or fourth effort. Second-mile Christians are a minority. Dropping out after the first lap will destroy your ego. Go for broke! Even if it "kills" you!

By the way, don't forget chapter 11. Yeah, it's okay, glance back at it. Then, last of all, be too gung-ho to wilt beneath the blistering heat of failure. Sigh deeply. Start again.

Think green!

In His Image:

I *can do everything through him who gives me strength* (Phil. 4:13).

You're Worth It!

Build *your Christ-confidence now:*

1. Try out positive daydreaming on a problem that scares you to death.

2. Think of something you would like to accomplish if you had absolutely no limitations—if you had unlimited money, talents, intelligence, and so on.
3. Reread the verse from Philippians again and explain why you can't accomplish the thing you thought of in #2.

14

It Must Be a Full Moon

Werewolf movies never scared me, and they still don't. In fact, I think they are a blend of comedy and Mutual of Omaha's "Wild Kingdom." The story is predictably the same. Some unfortunate guy has this nasty curse on him. When the moon is full he changes from his usual fun-loving self into a vicious, hairy half-man/half-wolf.

After several manglings, his girlfriend (all werewolves have girlfriends) pleads for help from a gypsy, a doctor (quack), or anybody willing to run the risk of becoming wolf food. At last, nothing works to remove the awful spell. Meanwhile, a full moon has made the wolfman stark raving mad, and he is about to rip his girlfriend into shreds.

Somehow he must be stopped! Lo and behold! The local werewolf bounty hunter discovers that only silver bullets will finish off the poor monster. It is always at this point that I expect the Lone Ranger—silver bullets and all—to come racing to the rescue on his trusted horse, Silver. He never does. But they shoot the werewolf anyway, just before he gobbles up the last living girl in the show. Then everybody cries (I laugh) when the corpse changes back into his real shape. The best part about the wolf's getting killed is that the movie is now over.

Being the expert on werewolf legend that I obviously am, I have made a startling discovery. Although I know your first response will be to think this is far-fetched, I am confident you will soon agree. Ready to hear my theory? *Puberty is a lot like becoming a werewolf.* That's all right—go ahead and laugh. See if you get any pity from me at the next full moon!

Here's my evidence:

Item #1: The arrival of hair all over the body. Sounds gross, but this is an inescapable truth of puberty. First on the legs, then under the arms. This starts never-ending agony for the girls. Over the years, the average woman will shave approximately 6,840 times, dulling about 2,829 razor blades! Guys just let theirs grow. In America hairy equals manly.

Item #2: The outbreak of stuff on the face. Not just whiskers. More specifically—zits! Like a mighty army, white-heads and blackheads pop up everywhere. The whole face and neck become a combat zone for three to five years. Blah!

Item #3: The sprouting of new physical features. During the teenage years, the body that began as a simple Volkswagen gradually develops into a Corvette. It's hormone city! The fountain of youth is springing forth into adulthood, and the newfound interest in the opposite sex is unmistakable. Full moon or not, romance begins to blossom. Guys especially start acting like wolves, if you know what I mean.

Item #4: The total absence of a cure. The only way to get rid of puberty is to live through it. Widespread as it is, no one has created an antidote. And there's a good reason why. God is using these difficult experiences to mature you. Before you know it, the whole thing will be over. One day you might even look back at it all and chuckle. For now, try to enjoy yourself. This is a special time of life; it can never be repeated in any way. Don't wish these years away!

See? I told you that puberty is a lot like becoming a werewolf. So be warned—your body will undergo many changes. Not even your voice is left alone! For the days when you hate this ordeal, let me leave you with one last insight. Get ready, because this is sort of sad. When high school is over and you receive that sacred diploma, the silver bullet will sink deep into your heart. You will slowly change into the adult you. Bittersweet as it is, you will be saying good-by to a huge chunk of your life—your childhood.

In His Image:

> And we, who with unveiled faces all reflect the Lord's glory, are being transformed into his likeness with ever-increasing glory, which comes from the Lord, who is the Spirit (2 Cor. 3:18).

You're Worth It!

Don't wait for a full moon before you answer one of these questions:

1. What is the hardest part of puberty for you?
2. What do you enjoy most about being a teenager?
3. Have you noticed any of your opinions or viewpoints changing as you mature? Name one or two.

15

Big Boys Don't Cry

David Seamands deciphers some truths about us, which we don't like to admit, in *Putting Away Childish Things*. He says that what we are now has a whole lot to do with the things we were taught as children. Some kids learn to express their emotions. They are taught that it's okay to laugh or cry aloud, to hug the people who are dear to you, or to speak up for yourself if another person is treating you like slime. They are encouraged to allow their emotions to be a part of their makeup and not be ashamed to show them.

Others are not taught this, usually because the parents themselves have serious trouble showing their feelings. So another batch of kids grows up to feel stifled in expressing themselves. Many times they would like to say or do something—anything—to let their feelings out, but they just don't know how. The longer this image is carved into a person, the harder it gets to be anything else.

This questionable honor is owed to the big-boys-don't-cry creed. That's the unwritten law that says, "People who show their emotions too readily are weaklings." Can I get upset here? Forgive me if I am failing to control myself, but that is the stupidest rule I've ever heard. Whoever thought it up should be tickled on the bottom of his feet until he is out of his mind with laughter. Then he should be told sad stories until he cries like a banshee. Okay, so I got a little carried away. But I did it to make a point: *Whenever something touches us down inside or upsets us, sometimes it is good to let it out.*

I'm not recommending that you become emotional dynamite—exploding upon any impact of joy or sorrow. You have probably met a few people like this. They cry at the tiniest tidbit of sadness. Or they spout off about everything that even remotely upsets them. Or they are so super-extroverted that they come off being loud and brash. You know the type. They wear their feelings on their sleeves, as the cliché goes.

The trick is to be somewhere in between cold, hard, and lifeless, and slushy, earsplitting, and unbearable. Here are a few ideas that might help:

1. **Don't** *be in control of your emotions*. What! Got you, didn't I? It was said that way on purpose, to get your attention. Let God hold the reins of your emotions. He will know best when they should gallop or just graze. He will keep you from feeling paranoid, revengeful, ultra-depressed, or unrestrained with love, or from pouting. By daily asking for the Holy Spirit's guidance in your emotions, you will start on the right track.

2. *Think through your emotions.* Those little critters of feeling can get you into trouble. Some people end up confused, way off base, and hurt, just because they let their sensitivity overpower them. Don't blurt out a reaction that hasn't been mulled over. And beware of imagining that a

hate campaign is being waged against you if Susie doesn't speak to you in the hallway today. When you get all riled up or sulky for nothing, it makes marks on your character and gives you the reputation of being an irrational or moody person. If you're like this, you will find yourself a good arm's length away from most people. This is not the best picture of you.

3. *Try expressing yourself at appropriate times.* During class discussions, speak up. You don't have to control the whole conversation, but you should never be afraid to toss in your two cents' worth. At Thanksgiving or Christmas, open up and share your sentimentality. Who cares if somebody thinks you're weak! It takes a special kind of bravery to show emotion in a considerate, tender, compassionate way.

Soon you will feel freer to express your disapproval of things that oppose godliness. You won't be ashamed to shed a tear when watching a touching program on TV. Out of the blue, you will get a notion to visit someone you care about in the hospital. Or send a card to cheer another. Or be friendly to people who have a hard time making friends— because they don't know how to express their feelings.

You will refashion a childish motto. Then perhaps other big boys and girls who are afraid to cry will finally grow up.

In His Image:

Jesus wept (John 11:35).

"In your anger do not sin": Do not let the sun go down while you are still angry, and do not give the devil a foothold (Eph. 4:26–27).

You're Worth It!

Sandblast the mortar that bricks in your emotions by branching out:

1. Try to write a loving poem for a family member (brother, sister, parent, grandparent).
2. Think of a time when you were really moved and

64

wanted to cry or tell how you felt, but didn't. Figure out what stopped you.

3. Talk to the Lord about your feelings and ask for his help to blend them into you, to fulfill the unique design he created you to be.

16

Secret "Blanket" Carriers

My little girl, Sara, carries a blanket. She can hardly imagine life without it. I'm not sure of exactly what that blanket possesses that gives her the added boost she needs to feel secure, but I know it has something. To deprive Sara of her blanket is the same as child abuse, in her opinion. She is three years old.

We are tickled a little bit by a child who carries around a security blanket, but the world is full of teenage and adult secret "blanket" carriers. Oh, not the regular chunk of cotton cloth the young ones tote. These are blankets of a different fabric. They are odd things we hang on to, hang-ups we have, that show our insecurity.

That's right. We display our insecurities in the plain view of all. How? Just to name a few: clinging to the same small group of friends, avoiding friendships altogether, putting a hand up over the mouth when smiling or talking, super-timid actions or extremely pushy ones, running other people down, a horrible temper, or conforming to wrong standards just to fit in. The list could go on.

However, insecurity is not a physical problem that can be healed with medicines and ointment. Oh, sure, we satisfy and cover our shilly-shally feelings with outer blankets. But, until things change on the inside, the quivers and shakes continue. The question is: Are you terribly insecure? I don't mean the normal fears most everybody feels. Do you depend heavily upon security blankets to keep you feeling warm as a person?

Let's play doctor. No, not *that* kind of doctor! Just plain old amateur psychologist. Don't worry, your head won't shrink. (Then again, I guess there are some heads big enough to need some shrinking.) By studying these principles you can diagnose any insecurity you may have:

Diagnosis #1: Insecure people like living in a small world. A vast circle is too threatening. The larger the world, the more vulnerable we become. There are more variables and a greater chance of being hurt. For a person who is fed up with heartache already, a smaller world is a safer world.

That is why every Linus (of Charlie Brown fame) sticks with a clique. Ranging outside of it to make new friendships is far too big an adventure. It might mean self-sacrifice. Personal goals, whims, interests, and happiness would have to be forgotten for a while. The insecure person couldn't have his snug world wrapped around him—protecting his fragile ego like a cottony blanket.

Spiritual medication: Base your security upon God, because he is in absolute control of all things. He is quite capable of working things out for your good. You can bravely walk with him into a bigger world, knowing that he will give meaning and purpose to every tiny detail that comes your way.

Diagnosis #2: Insecure people treat other people like things. They wish to own them and think they have exclusive rights to those people. Anyone who interferes is bound to be the brunt of a temper tantrum or slander session. It's a keep-your-hands-off-my-blanket retaliation. Why do they want to possess people? They are love-starved. I know, they have a funny way of showing it. But they are.

Behind insecurity are fears of being unwanted or unloved. That makes it easy to see why insecure people can be so ultra-possessive. They are afraid of being dumped, ditched, or double-crossed. Usually it has happened to them before, or maybe they have never really had a close friend.

Spiritual medication: Begin by building a strong friendship with Jesus Christ, because he never changes. He won't let you down; he's the same yesterday, today, and forever. Then ask the Lord to help you treat your friends with the same courtesy and love that God shows toward us.

Diagnosis #3: Insecure people have a powerful urge to be in charge. If they cannot have their own way, they will pout, be demanding, or turn their backs and walk away. When everything does not go according to plan, they can worry themselves crazy.

Since we brought up worry, it's a truth that insecure people are the super-worriers of mankind. They are just scared silly of losing control. If they are not boss, then who knows what awful things might happen to them? You see, behind insecurity is also mistrust. So they remain defensive, always watching out of the corners of their eyes for fear that someone might try to sneak up and steal their "blanket."

Spiritual medication: Let God be in control. He is anyway. Simply place your friendships or lack of them into his hands. God can then work in your life to give you the inner courage you need to become secure with him and yourself. You will no longer be in a frantic panic to hold life so tightly. Trust him!

We have a waterbed in our bedroom. I enjoy it immensely, especially when I wake up on a cold winter morning with the quilts pulled up to my nose. The water maintains a temperature of between 95 to 98 degrees, thanks to the built-in heater. So it's very cozy under those covers.

One problem: I can't stay in there all day, although there are times I'd like to. And to get out I've got to throw back the *blankets*. No matter how psyched up I get, the cold air pierces me at first.

Of this I am sure: If you have a "blanket" to put away, it won't be easy in the beginning. But you will gradually grow warmer in the comforting security of God's love. Throw back the blankets and climb out of insecurity's bed!

In His Image:

> *The name of the Lord is a strong tower; the righteous run to it and are safe* (Prov. 18:10).

You're Worth It!

Become better by developing spiritual security:

1. If a diagnosis in this chapter fits you, then try the "medication" suggested to heal it.
2. Invite new people into your circle of friends by being friendly toward them.
3. Memorize Proverbs 18:10.

17

Status Symbols

A popular television program exposes "The Lifestyle of the Rich and Famous." It portrays the affluent in fantastic luxury cars and highlights extravagant tidbits about renowned people. The series shows their multimillion-dollar homes, tells about the posh dining they can afford, reveals the huge expense of their clothing, lists their hangouts, and describes their playthings (planes, yachts, motorcycles, and so on).

About ten minutes is enough for me. Because the coverage seems to be aimed at making us "less important" people feel jealous about what they have that we don't—as though if only we could have those things, we too would be among the elite. Big deal! A human being's worth is not figured by what he's worth in currency or other possessions. It is determined by the value of life itself—the soul. That's priceless! Those two guys, "Rich" and "Famous," have nothing to do with self-worth.

But we are like that, aren't we? We tend to place people in categories. The greater their status, the better they seem. This silliness is age-old. Remember the caste system, the sad misfortune of being born into a certain class or rank of people and being stuck there for life? We do the same today with our so-called lower, middle, and upper classes. Except now it is possible to achieve higher status.

That makes self-esteem a status game to some people. Just get the status symbols that stand for "success" and become important. True? No, false. Genuine self-worth has absolutely nothing to do with wealth or fame. In fact, chew on this: *Humanly speaking, we are all a bunch of sinful, worthless wretches.* The value of a person rests solely in the love of God, who created us, desires our friendship, and goes to infinite lengths to wash away the sinfulness that taints our worth. Remarkable!

Therefore, there is no difference between rich or poor. Obviously, God does not think importance is measured by power and possessions, or else Jesus would have been born in a palace and would have grown up to become an earthly king. Although Jesus was poor, he definitely had no self-image problem. Can you imagine him worrying about getting recognized for outstanding achievement in public speaking? Can you see him comparing himself with John the Baptist to measure if he had reached the status quo for *The Who's Who of Israelite Preachers*? Ridiculous!

Think about it—teenagers have their own status symbols that imply "class." Naturally, anyone who successfully plays the status-symbol game is special. Anyone who doesn't is a loser. Right? Wrong. This stupid game is a way of becoming "important" (self-centered), which of course means higher "self-worth" (bigheaded conceit). I hope you're catching my sarcasm. Because status symbols are not a lasting way to build the best you. They more often than not lead to a keep-up-with-the-Joneses approach to life. Check out these status symbols and see what I mean:

Designer labels: We've gone crazy over alligators, initials, famous names, expensive brands, and the latest looks. Being somewhat fashion-conscious is no sin, but it shouldn't be the cement in building a person's worth.

Cars: Teenagers who have cars are thumbs up; teenagers who don't have them blend into the bland, tasteless, lifeless woodwork of life. Have your own car and instantly you are a somebody. Without wheels you're a nobody. Status symbols strike again. How meaningless!

Beauty: If you can get "oohed and ahhed" by other people, then you are worth something. Correct? Incorrect a third time. The structure of cheekbones, jawline, hairline, eye color, lip shape, dental arrangement, skin texture, and eyelash length surely can't decide worth. By the way, trying to look great isn't wrong. But founding self-worth upon looks is a tragic mistake.

Rings: Acceptance is something everyone likes, wants, and needs. Rejection is the pits, so going steady is supposed to be the perfect answer to always having someone to turn to. This is status—to have a boy friend or girlfriend to show off to everyone else. Does this really make anyone important?

Abilities or talents: Jocks and brains are the two high-school upper classes. Combining the two is to enter the truly elite group. Once again, there is nothing wrong with being a good athlete or a fine student. The mistake is in believing that those who don't reach this status are worth less.

Clubs: By belonging to the reputable school clubs, one can become recognized. Becoming a cheerleader is real status. National Honor Society is real status. Okay, fine. Shoot for these things. But don't be convinced that you're a zip if you can't achieve them. Worth does not equal status. Worth equals what value God gives you, which is equal to everyone else's—priceless! True worth is felt when we reach our God-given potential, not when we finally get noticed by other people. Reaching potential brings dignity; "getting noticed" brings only pride. Now *there* is a difference really worth discovering.

Status symbols come by the dozens. Some people spend a lifetime trying to feel better about themselves by achieving some higher level, and goals aren't bad in themselves. Goals can be helpful in challenging self-worth, for it is normal for a person who has developed a positive self-image to want to accomplish wonderful things. But it should not be the other way around—wanting to be called "important" because you finally get a brownie point.

Just believe that God values you. That puts you in a special class—a class where status symbols are not the measuring rod of value. Love is. How much is that? After the dollar sign comes a one and then an everlasting string of zeros. Bank on it!

In His Image:

Jesus said to them. . . . "For who is greater, the one who is at the table or the one who serves? It is not the one who is at the table? But I am among you as one who serves. . . . For he who is least among you all— he is the greatest (Luke 22:25, 27; Luke 9:46).

You're Worth It!

Spirituality overcomes status because it builds a deeper, truer, wiser you for the rest of life:

1. In your own words, tell what makes you an important person.
2. Have you been trying to gain status to feel more important? If so, what symbols have you been trying to earn?
3. What do you think about wealth, fame, and how they relate to self-worth?

18

Clown Tricks

Every class has a clown, or a corps of clowns. These people are constantly cracking a joke or performing some antic to get laughs. Schoolteachers know the clowns well and are often the target of their comical tricks. While the class roars at the sidesplitting gags, the teachers get a sudden urge to do some headsplitting.

Most teenagers aren't incurable pranksters or goof-offs. It takes a special brand of bravery to do that nutty stuff. But I wonder, is it really bravery? Is it ever rebellion? Or is it a cover? You know, a disguise. Do you think it is possible that the comedians at school go through their routines to hide the struggles they may be having with self-acceptance? Makes sense, doesn't it?

Sure, there's no better way to get attention—and we all like to be noticed—than to become a hilarious actor. Humor is appealing, and we usually like anybody who is able to put "life" into life. So clowning around is a natural way for some people to fit in.

However, underneath the funny disguise is often a person drowning in fears and self-doubt. I know that seems hard to believe, because when the jokester is at his hottest he appears to be very self-confident, completely at ease, and well liked. And yet, almost always there is another side to the class clown that hardly anyone sees.

Clowns have a sad and serious side. Of course, it is carefully guarded because it could stop the laughs if everyone thought he or she was battling growing up just like everybody else. To lose the laughter would be to take away the only true source of ego building that person has.

Some comics make themselves the brunt of their own jokes. This is especially done to ward off cutting remarks about slightly unusual physical features. For instance, a guy with a big nose might insist on making funny remarks about his own nose. He might even want a nickname like "Beak," "Schnoz," or "Birdman." He figures if he can get everybody busting up over his nose with his own wisecracks, then nobody will take pot shots at him, because they will already know that he thinks it's funny.

But guess what! When he is alone there are times when he wishes he didn't have that nose. He may even hate it. But he could never tell that to anyone. Then his nose would be fair game, and so would his feelings. So he just pretends to have it all under control. The same goes for a girl with big ears, big feet, or braces, or a guy with a short or scrawny frame.

Let me change direction for a minute. I think it's great to be comfortable enough with yourself to make jokes or laugh at kidding about some flaw in your old bod. People who can do this have achieved a level of self-acceptance unknown by many. It's too bad when we take ourselves so seriously that we can't have a good chuckle at our own imperfections. Sometimes this is just the ticket to take the edge off.

However, constantly beating oneself down to receive attention (laughs) eventually has its toll. Somewhere along the way the clown has got to come to grips with reality and accept it. That will keep the humor from becoming self-inflicted punishment for not being "normal."

The clown also needs to learn that life has its serious and sacred sides, too. And that they should not be mutilated with tasteless jokes. There are times when silence is superior to stupidity. Easy now, I'm neither a villain nor an ogre. Good times rate high on my list of favorite things. I'm just saying you should balance the clown act with calmness and good judgment. A dash of moderation never hurt anybody.

One last thing about clown tricks. I find that class comics get into an awful lot of trouble. Often they are poor readers and have other low grades as well. When they should be digging in to raise their skills, they are disrupting to raise the roof. Agree or not, this is bad news, and it has a payday coming.

Missing out on a much-needed education for laughter's sake is foolish. A tomorrow will come when school is over, and the clowns will then be painting on more permanent sad faces instead of happy ones, because they will not have the mental tools to improve themselves. Their troubles will just be beginning—a new, more complex bout with self-confusion—when the struggle for teenage self-worth will be coming to a close for the others who used to think that "Beak" had it all together.

But then "Beak" will have no crowd to tell his jokes to.

In His Image:

> There is a time for everything,
> and a season for every activity under heaven:
> . . . a time to weep and a time to laugh,
> a time to mourn and a time to dance,

a time to scatter stones, and a time to gather them,
a time to embrace and a time to refrain,
a time to search and a time to give up,
a time to keep and a time to throw away,
a time to tear and a time to mend,
a time to be silent and a time to speak....

Eccles. 3:1, 4–7

You're Worth It!

Now it's time for your feedback:

1. Do you have an odd physical feature? If so, are you able to laugh about it?
2. How far do you think joking around should go? What's the cutting-off point?
3. What does it mean to have a sense of humor? Do you have a good one?
4. Can you laugh with your parents? Do you ever share a funny joke or laugh at each other's blunders? When?

19

Pity-Parties

Self-pity is alive and well on Planet Earth. And it is a familiar ploy of all ages, as well as the most popular one-person party going. All people have thrown a pity-party in their own honor at least once. Haven't you? Be honest now.

Most folks do not recognize what causes self-pity. Do you? Think about it for a while. Self-pity sometimes crops up when our expectations are not met or when a circumstance causes our plans to be delayed. It may surface when we get mistreated or even when a tool we need breaks down or some other bad thing happens to us. So what's really behind self-pity? If you said "anger" you are correct.

Self-pity is anger turned outside in. Instead of blowing their tops, pity-party people will dash off to their bedrooms to mope and feel sorry for themselves—"Poor, poor me!"

They may even forge ahead with a temper fit, then change into their self-styled sackcloth and ashes.

Isn't this embarrassing? I mean, since we have all acted out this dumb little charade, do you feel as red-faced as I do about being so childish? I can see mental replays of myself—pouting and thinking, "Nobody thinks about me and my feelings. All they care about is themselves." And why shouldn't they, since all I cared about was myself!

That's the fine print about self-pity that nobody reads. It translates as pure selfishness. Here's more of the fine print. Read it before you sign the contract to have your next pity-party:

It is never enough to erase the problem.

It makes things worse than they really are.

It drives people away instead of drawing them closer.

It makes you more miserable.

It is a cover-up for your own faults.

It doesn't add one thing to your favor.

It encourages you to be irresponsible.

It leaves you feeling empty.

Don't you see? This is only a substitute for self-worth. Those who rest secure in the Lord as their Guardian have no need to use this technique to protect themselves from the cuts and bruises of life. That may sound easy, but it isn't. I don't know about you, but pain is not my idea of a good time.

Then again, experience teaches me that pity-parties aren't much fun either. When I used to dally with the see-how-neglected-I-am game, it was a super-downer. My valleys were never lower, and the shadows were never darker. Instead of making me stronger, it made me weaker and caused my self-worth to ebb to low tide.

Here are some of the reasons why self-pity hurts you more than it helps you:

1. *You will want to blame somebody else.* It's the if-it-hadn't-been-for-them-parade. It must be somebody else's fault that "success" did not come. Self-pity begs you to say to yourself, "See, you are not really to blame; they are. Now no one can hold you responsible, because it wasn't your fault." Oh, Mr. Self-Pity is a persuasive talker. Just listening to him will have you believing you never need to apologize and you don't really need to change—other people are the ones who need changing.

2. *You will want to give up on yourself.* Self-pity starts talking to you again and says, "You are an oaf. You never do anything right. Just don't try anymore, then no one will pick on you. Now go ahead—feel sorry for yourself. It isn't your fault, but it's useless to keep trying. Stay here with me. Let's enjoy each other's miserable company." Those may not be the exact words, but self-pity is bent on isolating you from anyone or anything.

3. *You will want to feel helpless.* Of course you will, because that brings you much-needed sympathy from other people. Have you seen the special look that self-pity has? It's a please-notice-me-and-feel-sorry-for-me expression. I think it's sickening. Jonah-types ought to wake up before they get the royal fishing lesson of their lives.

4. *You will want to manipulate others.* Self-pity makes you out to be the martyr and tries to make others feel guilty if they don't do something to help you. Neat trick, huh? For a while maybe, but pretty soon they catch on and run the opposite way when they see you coming.

Pity, pity, pity! In a way I do feel very sorry for the pity-partiers because they are the real losers. Their dignity is being slimed, and their integrity is being beheaded. What a mess they become, a distant cry from the blueprint God drafted.

I guess you could call me a pity-party-pooper.

In His Image:

My tears have been my food day and night. . . . Why are you downcast,
O my soul? Why so disturbed within me? Put your hope in God, for I
will yet praise him, my Savior and my God (Ps. 42:3, 5).

You're Worth It!

Reach out and win over that inner voice that begs you to withdraw:

1. Have you wallowed in self-pity lately? If so, over what?
   Did it really do any good?
2. What should we do whenever we are treated unfairly?
   Should we strike back? What does God's Word say?
3. If you have a friend mired down in self-pity, let him or
   her read this chapter.

20

BMOC

If you are wondering what those letters stand for, I'll give you a clue: It isn't Bigmouth the Official Celebrity, although in some cases that would fit just as well. BMOC is short for Big Man on Campus. I guess a girl is called a VIP (Very Important Person), since BGOC might not be too flattering.

What we're chatting about here is popularity. Popularity usually works like a balloon—it fills the head with hot air until it either floats away into the clouds or else pops! Few people can handle an overabundance of attention and praise.

Most teenagers would give their eyeteeth to have the chance at such a dilemma. On the outside, being the chosen idol at school looks glamorous. Having the girls—if you're a guy—fainting over you, as they wait in line to touch your hand, is like a fantasy. For girls, it is wish number one from Aladdin's lamp to be chased by the cutest, most sought-after guys. This is the kind of popularity the average red-blooded American teenager dreams of.

So why do I have to go and ruin a good thing? I guess I like to meddle. So here goes. Please stay with me on this one, because you will agree with me before I'm finished. I promise you!

To get the ball rolling, let's clear up one cockeyed idea. How popular a person is in school is not a yardstick for value. It is mindless to base something as serious as a person's worth upon the ups and downs of popularity.

Example: Let's say you are well liked. Does that make you any better than anybody else? No. Agreed? Of course not. All right then, let's reverse that. If someone is more popular than you, does that make him or her better? Ah-ah-ah! Don't hesitate on me now. No, that does not make them more significant—not one iota.

Why, then, do we make such a rigamarole out of this superstar stuff? Why do we play comparison games? Why do we intimidate ourselves into thinking we're nobodies if we don't attract huge crowds of friends?

You probably think I'm against being popular. No, not at all. It's just that I've had the rare privilege of being on both ends of the stick, several times. And I can verify that I was exactly the same Brent Earles during my unpopular periods as I was during my popular times. For the most part, nothing about me changed.

People tend to be fickle. Have you noticed that? For instance, when it's fall and football is the craze, the star half-back is getting admired by everybody. Except for 6'3" "Joe," down in the gym shooting hoops. In a few months the half-back will be a memory and "Joe" will be the hero.

Get this, in a side room "Laurie" is paying no attention to the cheerleading squad. She could make it, if she wanted.

But she is studying. Her shining moment will come in a couple of years when she is named valedictorian.

Believe me, the people who are popular today aren't always so hot tomorrow. It is much better to concentrate on being a steady, consistent, dependable person than to ride the tidal waves of cheap and easy applause. Sure, you should try to be well liked, because that means you have developed your personality in positive ways. These types are always respected by their peers, because they are kind and unselfish.

That brings me to another point. Have you been a witness to what popularity does to some people? It can turn them into proud peacocks. They strut around with their noses up in the sky as if afraid they might smell somebody less cool than themselves. Hey! It could happen to you. Or it may be happening to you now. Take inventory.

Being popular has its advantages. So does beauty. And brawn. And brains. And breeding. However, none of these things determines the value or potential of a person. Not everyone can become a BMOC or VIP. But they can become UTTL. UTTL? Yes—Useful to the Lord.

That's better than Bigmouth the Official Celebrity any day of the week.

In His Image:

> [Jesus said:] "If the world hates you, keep in mind that it hated me first. If you belonged to the world, it would love you as its own" (John 15:18–19).

You're Worth It!

Become UTTL *by building on your spiritual foundations:*

1. How can a Christian cope with popularity? Is it wrong to seek it?
2. Ask your parents whether either of them was popular

in high school. Have them share how they felt about popularity.

3. Write down four major goals you have for life. Then think about how popularity could help you reach them. You might find out what is meant by the phrase "stepping on people to get to the top." You might also find that noble goals don't need popularity's help to be achieved.

21

A Chapter for Upstream Swimmers

Salmon don't get a lot of headlines. Yet they are not your ordinary fish. Salmon swim *upstream* to find spawning grounds for reproduction. Don't ask me why they have to be so odd. I don't know why they can't just be like all the other fish. Unless! Unless God designed that instinct in them to teach us some valuable lessons. Like not letting the fast-flowing undercurrent sweep you away, not giving in to the churning waters that seem out to get you, not being beaten by the odds, being strong-willed enough to face troubled waters.

Not everybody has to swim upstream. Some people have it easier than others. But having it "easy" is no guarantee. In fact, those with all the advantages often take life for granted and end up on the devil's hook. And, oddly, just like the salmon, the ones with far fewer advantages many times overcome life's obstacles to become masterpieces in God's gallery.

How about Helen Keller? She was deaf, blind, and mute, but became one of history's finest humanitarians. She even overcame her muteness! Franklin D. Roosevelt was crippled. Booker T. Washington triumphed over racial discrimination. Babe Ruth was orphaned. Abraham Lincoln was very poor. King David of Israel started as a sheepherder. Ludwig van Beethoven suffered deafness at age twenty-eight, but went on to compose some of history's greatest music. His piano is still in existence, but it can't be played. He wore it out by pounding so hard trying to hear his own music. Jesse Owens ran "white supremacy" right down Adolf Hitler's throat at the 1936 Olympics in Germany by winning four gold medals. Naval Lieutenant Kennedy mastered heroics in time to save himself and crew members when a Japanese destroyer rammed his PT boat. He carved an SOS message on a coconut, which was carried by natives to rescuers. This brave officer was called Jack by close friends, but the world remembers him as John F. Kennedy, president of the United States during the "Camelot" days at the White House.

Maybe you think God has given you a raw deal. As a result, perhaps you have stopped trying. You may have started to give up on yourself and your future. I've seen the symptoms in those who are allowing the tough circumstances of life to get the best of them. The insecure, broken self-image of these people shows up most clearly in their emotions:

They carry a chip on their shoulder. This person often comes off as being obnoxious, hateful, or smart-mouthed. Anger eats away at the insides, while bitterness grows its long, cruel roots. The causes are various. Perhaps his mother died when he was a child . . . her parents were divorced when she was six . . . she had to have a leg amputated . . . he had an eye punctured accidentally... he has a "minority" heritage... her face was scarred badly in a fire... he is a paraplegic. It's upstream all the way for people like this, and rather than attempt to fight the tides of life, they fight life itself! They let hate grow down deep—a hate that ruins the beauty God has prepared for them. This hostility about being farther downstream than everybody else is an effort to appear strong, tough, macho. To cover feelings of pain. Instead of building a good image, a spiteful attitude drives other people away. This person ends up insincere, rough on people, and down on life.

They punish themselves with failure. Self-worth is demolished when a person dwells on bad circumstances. This person says to self, "You are no good. Look at all the problems you have. You'll never be worth anything. You weren't meant to be happy. You're a born loser. What's the use in trying? Everything is against you." This person ends up insensitive, short on hope, and down on self.

They listen to the voices of fear. These voices say things like: "It will hurt too much if you try that." "Think of all the sacrifices you will have to make." "People will laugh at you." Given enough rope, this fear will hang them from a gallows fashioned from withdrawal and isolation. Run away; that's the answer. Just ignore the gnawing hurt on the inside. Becoming a zombie is their choice. Mill around school in a depressed daze and lock people out. Avoid any risk. Float downstream. This person ends up insensible, afraid of trying, and down on tomorrow.

Let me straighten out one thing right now. I don't have answers for all the miserable situations that happen to people. I can't explain why God designs certain people with what appear to be tough breaks. I know that much of the pain in life is the result of sin. I also know that whatever the hindrance, God can bring the one who trusts him to victory. I know that this is his plan and desire.

God is not evil in any way. He does not send what we call suffering in order to injure someone, nor is he partial. God does not choose one person over another by making life "easier" for his favorites. If that were so, then Jesus wouldn't have been born a poor carpenter's son in Bethlehem's slums—a stable manger.

But I don't have to have all the answers. Neither do you. Neither does anybody else. Each of us has a choice to make, regardless of what comes our way: Are we going to become that unique person God is handcrafting us to be? Or are we going to allow hurdles to become permanent barriers?

A relationship with Jesus Christ is not the title deed to a rose-garden walk in life, but it is the backbone to the strength for upstream swimming.

Thank you, Lord, for sending your encouragement from the beginning, from creation—the salmon.

In His Image:

> . . . *genuine, yet regarded as imposters . . . known, yet regarded as unknown; dying, and yet we live on; beaten, and yet not killed; sorrowful, yet always rejoicing; poor, yet making many rich; having nothing, and yet possessing everything* (2 Cor. 6:8–10).

You're Worth It!

Fight the currents and swim into one of the following:

1. Do an in-depth study of the salmon. Begin with an encyclopedia.
2. Write down your greatest obstacle and pray daily for God's help to win over it.
3. Read the biography of one of the "upstream swimmers" mentioned at the beginning of this chapter.

22

The Guilt Complex

My dad is impossible to please," the student snapped. "No matter how well I do in school, my grades aren't good enough. Once I got all A's except for chemistry. I've never been great at science. I got a B−. When Dad saw it, did he say 'good job' for the A's? No, never. All he could talk about was that B−. To him I had committed the unpardonable sin!"

Frequently, teenagers battle with inner feelings that tell them they don't measure up. That say, "You're not quite good enough." They think they are a cut below the rest— that a tiny mistake makes them a total failure and that unless they are flawless, they are lousy.

You might think this strikes only the dropout, but if you do, you are wrong. This happens most often to the ones who appear to have all the ingredients of the ideal adolescence. I know that sounds weird, but it's true.

For example, here's a guy who everybody figures has it all together. He's better-than-average looking. Good grades come naturally for him. With letters in three sports and medals on his letter jacket, he is one of the superstars. Girls chase him everywhere. Last month he was elected class president. And he recently received a scholarship to a well-known university. But few people know how hard he is on himself. He nit-picks at himself and tells himself that he fails to measure up. His self-spun web of guilt keeps him from truly enjoying God's blessings in his life. In spite of wonderful achievements, he continues to feel empty and unsatisfied as a person.

A second case in point. A pretty blonde cheerleader is envied by others who wish everything would come up roses for them, too. She is bright and is first in her class. Guys follow her and give her all the attention she could ever need. Everybody supposes she will be a perfect success in life, but they don't know that many things secretly threaten her happiness. She feels super-pressured to be the image of perfection. And no matter how noble her efforts, she knows she could never live up to the expectations people have set for her. So her special accomplishments are lost in the mad rush to be better and better and better! Pure misery. Well hidden, but very much alive.

Is this happening to you? Do you demand so much of yourself that you are unable to be grateful for God's riches in your life? Have you drummed up some fantasy image to measure up to? Do you have to have things just so? When someone teases you, do you take mental notes and inwardly vow to correct whatever you were teased about? Do you compare yourself unfavorably with others? Are bad experiences at the center of your thoughts?

Well, we all want to succeed. To feel competent. Nobody wants to feel like a flop. But measuring up to God's standard is what spells *real* SUCCESS.

S— Surrender to the Holy Spirit. Begin each day with a simple prayer, asking the Lord to take control of your life for his glory.

U— Unload old saddles. Unbuckle old saddles you once used to ride yourself. Run bareback. It beats being on your own back all the time.

C— Check your emotions. Watch out for excessive negative thinking. Don't listen to the inner voices that used to drag you down.

C— Channel your ambitions. Don't live only for self. Empty yourself into serving others and pleasing God. Selfless people are successful people. (See Matt. 20:25–27.)

E— Echo Christ. Seek to reflect the image of Christ in your lifestyle. Don't be so concerned with your own image, but with the Lord's image in you.

S— Set reasonable goals. He who aims at nothing hits it every time. But aiming for Jupiter or Pluto is just as senseless. Shoot for goals you can reach by working hard.

S— Stay original. Losing your own identity while attempting to satisfy everyone else's expectations will frustrate you. Be yourself. Be the person God made you to be. That's plenty to live up to.

I think I should also mention that some guilt complexes are the fruit of sinful actions. When a person rejects Jesus Christ and lives rebelliously apart from purity, then guilt is a normal response for the conscience. Some people are lazy and/or reckless and don't want to give an account for their prodigal ways. They're heavily into making excuses, anything to get themselves off the hook. Guilt might be the best they can hope for.

It's a crazy world. Some people break their necks to "be

somebody," but never feel as if they make it. Others think they are already somebody," but they haven't done a thing. It's all because we are basically selfish and self-centered at heart. Yielding to Jesus Christ ends this foolish charade. You'll never have to measure up to empty standards again.

For, let me ask, who can measure up to *grace*?

In His Image:

Your attitude should be the same as that of Christ Jesus (Phil. 2:5).

You're Worth It!

Measure the influence one of the following devotions could have on your life. Then do it!

1. Confess your greatest weakness to someone you can really trust (parent, youth pastor, very trustworthy friend) and have this person pray with you.
2. Think of a few goals you would like to reach before graduation. Dream big enough to challenge yourself. Then go for it, starting now.
3. Think about rebellion. What causes it? How does it show itself? What can be done to remedy it? Are compromises always necessary?

23

Never Say "Never" Again

The *power of positive thinking*. Is that stuff for real? Does it have anything to do with self-worth? Does it apply to teenagers? Do you think some people get just a little carried away with it?

There are hordes of possibility thinkers flooding the bookshelves and airwaves. They all preach from a similar soap box: "You can—if you think you can." Got any gripes about that?" Only one thing bugs me about it. I believe that some of the possibility experts emphasize the power of self above the indispensable power of Christ. When that is straightened out, then even I can be found playing the positive-thinker game.

My goal in this chapter is to make you believe that you can become the person you were meant to be. To gear this high-brow, positive-thinking jive to the world of teenagers.

To make you believe in miracles again. To make "never" a word you use only to reject truly negative things.

Why do I want to stick a chapter like this in this book? Because *you're worth it*! You have got to begin believing that. God does. "Humility" isn't thinking you are worthless; it is finding your true worth in God alone. In becoming a special part of his creation, becoming a shining ray of his glory.

"Impossible" needs to become a word impossible for you to say. Because negative thinkers usually have a poor self-image and worse—a poor God-image. The God of the negative thinkers is too small. He's boxed in. Limited. Their God doesn't listen to prayer if the requests are super-big. Negative thinkers make their God give up, because *they* have given up on him. God rarely brings the miraculous to the negative know-it-alls, because they say he can't. The problem is not with God; it's with them. So, if you're ready, let me teach you to never say "never" again:

Build hotels on faith. If you think Boardwalk and Park Place pay big dividends in the Monopoly game, invest your worth in faith and see the fantastic dividends it pays in life. You will find that it unlocks the cage of gloom that hampers so much of teenage changing. The seemingly impossible struggles that you are "never" going to live through suddenly become islands in the stream. My favorite part of the possibility game is faith, because I know Jesus wants me to believe nothing is impossible.

By-pass pessimism's jail cell. Just as the worst place to land in Monopoly is "Go to Jail," the worst place to be in the possibility game is behind the bars of thumbs-down thinking. When I was in high school I had a goal: I wanted to be the speaker at my graduation ceremonies. When I was a sophomore I watched a friend graduate and decided that night that my destiny was to speak at my own commencement. One problem was that the school tradition was to have the valedictorian address the class. Now, my grades were pretty good, but I wasn't going to make valedictorian, because I had already blown it in one of my classes. But I still believed. Anyway, by the time I was a senior, the school decided to change the policy. Since our chapter of the National Honor Society had been so active, the faculty decided to have a speech-making contest. The two winners would speak. I competed with several others of my Honor Society comrades. And, yes, I won. But the story doesn't end there. On graduation night, after my speech, my grandfather put his arm around my shoulder and said, "Brent, you ought to become a preacher." I thought that was hilarious, because I certainly didn't want to be one of those. And it was odd that he should say such a thing, for no one in our family at that time was remotely near being such a thing. One year later I surrendered to God's leading to enter the ministry! I wonder if it would have been the same if I had given up as a sophomore! You see, pessimism doesn't stop us only today; it affects the whole future.

Be sure to pass "Go." Unless you pass "Go," you cannot collect your two hundred dollars. Right? Well, it's the same in the possibility game. If you don't get in the program and go with it, you won't get anywhere. Some people think big and dream big, but act small. When it comes to talk and plans they sound like Superman or Wonder Woman. But when it comes to performance it's Alibi City. Remember, just as important as faith is action. Faith without works is dead. Latch onto that, and you can turn possibilities into probabilities.

What would you like to accomplish in high school? High grades? Honor Society? Cheerleader? Football team captain? Class president? First chair in band? Pass geometry? Be a spiritual leader? Win writing awards? Sing solos in musical programs? Speak at special class events? *What do you really want to do?* What goals would fulfill you as a person during this time of your life?

We need a whole generation of positive thinkers—people

with faith in God so deep that it makes them try harder than ever. So start now by reaching out to capture that piece of your teenage destiny. It's the beginning of becoming the best you!

And never say "never" again.

In His Image:

> [The Lord says:] "Call to me and I will answer you and tell you great and unsearchable things you do not know" (Jer. 33:3).

> Jesus looked at them and said, "With man this is impossible, but with God all things are possible" (Matt. 19:26).

You're Worth It!

Stop saying "never" and do one of these:

1. Name two things that you have dreamed of doing in high-school, but thought were impossible. Then start playing the possibility game.
2. Put a rubber band around your wrist (one that fits loosely), and snap it each time you think negative, pessimistic thoughts during the day. Or snap it when you are thinking positively. Either way, it will make you more aware of how you think.
3. Think about what role physical, spiritual, and mental limitations play in the possibility game.

24

Stop Underpricing Yourself!

Someone has said:

We are not what we think we are...
We are not even what *others* think we are...
We are what we *think* others think we are.

Heavy stuff, huh? But there is a big message of truth in it. Each of us weighs how we think other people see us, and then we live out the character role they have created for us. We fall into the mold others have stereotyped for us.

For instance, take a girl who is overweight. She believes that people at school think her to be less of a person because she is heavy. She has been told that she is fat and clumsy, that she doesn't look good in her clothes, and that she is dumb. Gradually, she begins believing the mean remarks she has had to hear. Without knowing it, she lets these cruelties shape her individuality. She becomes very self-conscious. She refuses to participate in any athletic competition. She chooses to wear only the fashions that are designed for "fat people." And she becomes the silent type in order to avoid attracting attention. The insults continue, and she continues to fill the mold of an overweight person.

Now let me show you something. Take the same girl and put her in a situation where her self-esteem is not beaten to death. Although she feels awkward about her weight, her friends convince her to join Pep Club. Her personality begins to bubble. As soon as she begins to realize that people accept her, she feels freer to be herself. With self-confidence building, she decides to try out for the school play. She wins a part and does well in it. People genuinely like her. She becomes stronger and attacks her weight problem with a self-felt willpower, not because of the pressure to be skinny that the rest of the world puts on overweight people.

In both examples the girl becomes what she believes other people think her to be. If they reject her, she rejects herself and becomes worse off. If they accept her, she accepts herself and develops into a more confident person.

Here's the catch: There will always be both groups of people—those who appear to be against you and those who appear to be for you. It would be Disneyland if everyone always encouraged you and never made you feel worthless, even in the slightest way. And here's another point to ponder: Sometimes you will imagine that others are rejecting you when they really are not. It will be you underpricing *yourself*.

Once you really begin believing in yourself—believing that you are truly worth it—then you won't have to depend upon the good guys to wear white hats all the time. You won't have to be patted and stroked and bragged about. At the same time, when stinging jabs of criticism come your direction, your self-esteem will act as a force field to ward off any penetrating put-downs that threaten to mold you into a lesser person.

Don't get me wrong. No one ever comes to a place where he or she no longer needs to feel accepted by others. All of us need to feel that someone else believes in us. And few people ever reach a point where unkind blabbermouths are unable to hurt them with trashy, slimy words of rejection. My point is that when you believe in yourself the way that God believes in you, then your self-image and self-acceptance will no longer depend upon how you think other people view you. You will finally accept yourself just as you are. You will stop underestimating yourself just because somebody else undervalues you. And you will become better and better once you know you are accepted by God.

I'm making your brain sizzle, I know. It's probably about ready to overheat, because some of this stuff is tough to sift through. But I'm not going to let you off that easy. I'm not going to let you get away with thinking that this is too much mumbo jumbo for you to understand. If you didn't grasp it all, then back up and read it again! This is *you* we're talking about! And you are important. Right? Careful, though, don't get cocky.

Let me ask you three questions. Question number one: *How do you think most people see you?* Question number two: *How do you see yourself?* Question number three: *Are you underpricing yourself because of how others treat you?*

Get hold of this! If you have accepted Jesus Christ as your Savior, then you are a child of God. You belong to him, and he is committed to your growth as a person. The value he places on you is your true worth, for he is the only one capable of measuring a person's value. God says you're priceless! What do you say to that?

Maybe we should change that little ditty at the beginning of the chapter to say:

We are not what we think we are . . .

We are not even what *others* think we are . . .

We are not even what we *think* others think we are . . .

We are what we allow God to make us to be!

In His Image:

Accept one another, then, just as Christ accepted you, in order to bring praise to God (Rom. 15:7).

You're Worth It!

Invest in yourself by doing one of the following:

1. Write a paragraph answering these questions: What makes a person valuable? Are value and worth the same thing? Can a person decrease his or her value? Worth?

2. Talk to your dad about how he became his own person. Ask him if people ever tried to convince him that he was nobody. (You might ask your mom the same question.)

3. Think about how Jesus responded to people when they tried to hurt him and stop him through rejection. Was he tough? Tender? Did he bend? Fight back? Stand his ground?

25

Nobody Does It Better

Let's get down to the nitty-gritty. Some cold, hard facts. I'll just blurt it out: "You are not good at some things!" Feel better? We finally cleared the air on that subject. I mean, you have read through twenty-four chapters of locker-room pep talk that was beginning to make you think you didn't have any weaknesses after all.

So I finally said it, but you have been thinking it all along. Haven't you? You have been wanting to say, "Listen, Earles, if you give me another one of those Knute Rockne, win-one-for-the-Gipper speeches again, I'm gonna give this book to my dog to chew on!" Right?

Now the cat is out of the bag—you are not good at some things. Want to get down to the real nitty-gritty? At some things you are plain rotten. Okay? So we agree. At some things I am rotten. That makes us even.

Like golf. This sport is not my gig. My mother-in-law beats me at golf. Do you know how humiliating it is to be beaten at golf by your mother-in-law? What's worse, I fudge when she isn't looking. I pretend not to remember how many putts I took; I move my ball out of the rough when she looks the other way; I subtract strokes from the scorecard. And still she beats me! It's pretty safe to say that Jack Nicklaus and Tom Watson won't have to worry about me tearing up the pro circuits.

Singing is another of my horror stories. Talk about visions of grandeur, when it comes to singing I have them. Just put on a record or flip on the radio, turn up the volume loud enough to drown me out and make me "sound good," and I suddenly become a tremendous singer. In the shower, where echo and water noise provide all the sound distortion I'll ever need, my talents are "unequaled" (I guess that's one way of saying it). Honestly, where music is concerned, I'm at my best when I just sit and listen.

Mechanical abilities? Me? That's a laugher, too. Oh, I can take things apart like a champion—unscrew this, unfasten that, snap this little dilly-bob off, just pop that thing-a-ma-jig around, yank here, yank there, and bend this. Eventually, there are 119 tiny pieces scattered on the table and I haven't got the slightest idea what the problem is. Nothing ever goes back together for me, so I throw the mess away and buy a new one.

But I'm not lousy at everything. Nobody beats me at Monopoly. I am the Monopoly champion of the civilized world. No brag, just fact. Poetry and anything with words are fun for me, too. God has given me both a love and a knack for writing-related things. That, of course, is part of his design for me. Also, my wife says I would have made an excellent attorney because I can argue stubbornly. She rarely gets a word in edgewise, so she says.

Seriously speaking, for a moment. I don't claim to be the

greatest at anything I do. That's not my objective anyway, since I've nothing to prove. But I am thankful for the interests and abilities God has given me, and I plan to develop and use them fully. God wants me to please him by allowing him the freedom to work through the strengths and weaknesses he gave me. In the meantime, I can learn and grow in Christ.

My own strengths and limitations are like yours. In fact, we all have them. That's my point. So what if you're terrible at English or football or at playing an instrument. Maybe you have gifts in baseball or speech or singing. Whatever it is that you do well, keep doing it. Work at it. Practice. Become as good as you possibly can. Then do it for the Lord's honor throughout your life.

Instead of dwelling on how you wish you were as proficient at such-and-such a thing as so-and-so is, concentrate on what you are good at. Instead of putting yourself down because you aren't as popular as you would like to be, put your extra time into earning your wings at your own special talent.

A guy in our town did what I'm saying. His name was Jeff. He wasn't great at much, and he wasn't popular. But every afternoon when school got out Jeff was on the asphalt basketball court out behind our gymnasium. All alone. Taking shot after shot into the chain net and loose hoop on that metal backboard, Jeff went nearly unnoticed. Day after day the "shortie" practiced. For three years. Then his hour came. He was the starting point guard on the varsity basketball squad as a junior, and as a senior Jeff won conference, city, and state honors. Not bad for a guy who was too off-key to be in band.

But I wonder about one thing. Could he beat my mother-in-law at golf?

In His Image:

> For we are God's workmanship, created in Christ Jesus to do good works, which God prepared in advance for us to do (Eph. 2:10).

You're Worth It!

Become even better by joining in one of these projects:

1. Write down your bad points, poor subjects, and so on, and spend the whole next month working to better yourself in these areas.
2. Think of a way you could use your talents to serve the Lord, and begin by trying to do what you can right now.
3. Make a list of the physical, mental, and spiritual gifts or talents the Lord has given you. Then say a prayer of thanks to him, dedicating yourself to use those things only to honor him.

26

Finish the Job

Y̶ou may not realize it, but here comes one of the most important lessons to be learned if you want to become your very best self. It's not a fancy lesson. It isn't glamorous. It isn't even appealing. After years of going undiscovered and unlearned by the masses, it has grown a bit dusty. The message is simple and cannot be improved upon: FINISH WHAT YOU START.

Let's-only-go-halfway-then-let's-quit enthusiasts give me stomach cramps. And after a while they get pretty sick of themselves, too. In time they even lose their energy for starting new projects, because they know they never finish anything. Why start something you will never finish? So they bum out. And any combination of the following attitudes begins to show up:

The Who-Cares? Attitude. This one flips its nose at anything that demands responsibility and perseverance. Often it is displayed by sagging grades, frequent bouts with authority, common laziness, a loss of motivation, skipping classes or being regularly late, refusing to put forth genuine effort, sloppy appearance, and even dropping out altogether.

The You-Owe-Me Attitude. It acts as if the whole world has a debt to pay, and it owes that debt to one person—*me!* At heart, people with this outlook believe others should finish the job for them, since they can't (won't!) finish it for themselves. This is shown by those who constantly leave their responsibilities for parents to do. (For example, "Straighten my bed; clean up my room; take out the garbage for me; wash the car for me; mow the lawn, I'm busy; tidy the kitchen table, I'm watching TV.") These types end up nowhere, for they are quite satisfied to wait forever for someone else to get them there.

The I'm-Helpless Attitude. This says, "Woe is me! I tried, honest I tried, but I just can't finish it. Please finish it for me. I would be so grateful. You could do it so much better than I ever could. Poor me. If only I were able." Pardon me, but I sometimes want to konk these types on the noggin. There's nothing wrong with these people that a strong dose of guts and grit couldn't cure.

The There's-Always-Tomorrow Attitude. Big plans. Long on talk, with enough hot air to fill all the balloons at a national convention. But no work until . . . tomorrow. Of course, tomorrow never comes. Talk is cheap. For that matter, starting is fairly cheap. I mean, most anybody can get off to a rip-roaring start. What you hear little about are rip-roaring finishers. Instead, "I'm gonna finish that just as soon as I get to it," they say. To which I reply, "Yes, and that is what makes me so nervous."

Let me level with you, finishing things you start is no picnic. It takes stamina. Believe me, it takes stamina. Perhaps nothing illustrates my point better than writing a book. Oh, at first it is so exciting, what with the ideas flowing and all.

Suddenly, the halfway marker is reached—better known as Dead Man's Land. All the words seem to be the same. Chapters fade into other chapters. I ask myself, "Does this make any sense? Who cares about this, anyway? Will anybody read this? Am I wasting my time? Is it going to take forever to finish this?" Then, if I can survive that long stretch of chapters between the first one and the last, I know I can finish.

Most tough and rewarding projects are like that. They sap every bit of your energy to get finished. However, they refill your fuel tank with plenty of gallons of satisfaction and fulfillment.

You need to finish the things you start, or else you are bound to become an underachiever. Don't you think it would be difficult to live with yourself and look at yourself in the mirror, day after day, if you knew you weren't living anywhere near up to your potential? You might come to hate yourself.

You see, accomplishment is the father of dignity. Achievement builds the proper aspects of your ego when you finish a worthwhile project—a sort of "healthy pride." It makes you *feel* as if you are worth something. Knowing that God says you are valuable is one thing; it is an altogether different matter to *feel* valuable because of a finished project.

Don't get lost in Dead Man's Land. It takes no prisoners. Just drag yourself through, somehow, to the end—the finish line. Then look up to heaven and see who carried you most of the way.

In His Image:

Lazy hands make a man poor, but diligent hands bring wealth (Prov. 10:4).

You're Worth It!

Finish *one* of these:

1. Talk to someone who has graduated and ask whether he or she thinks high school went by fast.

2. Think of a project you started but haven't finished. Start working on it again until it is done.
3. Can you think of two or three things you started, worked on, and finished? Are they a source of "healthy pride"?
4. Read Proverbs 10:4. Consider the two words *poor* and *wealth*. What could they mean, besides money or material possessions?

27

Hints on Camera Breaking

Could anyone ever be so ugly that taking his or her picture could actually break a camera? I doubt it. At least, I've never heard of it. However, there are some things that cannot be hidden by professional photography. Even drastic touch-up work can't cover some flaws.

No, I'm not talking about blemishes and scars. Or plain ugliness. Because physical beauty isn't all that shows up in pictures. Other things can be visible as well. Things like sadness, unhappiness, toughness, pain, bitterness, and confusion. Oh, sure, the pros can fool the eye by using tricky techniques, but they can't change the eyes of the person being photographed. Many times the eyes can say so much. And although I wouldn't place a lot of stock in picture-reading judgments of people, as an avid amateur photo buff I know that deep emotion can be captured on film.

I also know that otherwise wonderful people have "ug-lied" themselves with *self*-destructive living. Gradually, it shows in all they do, and they cannot hide it. Bit by bit they ruin themselves—from the inside out. When God turns to point his spiritual Polaroid in their direction to catch a snapshot of their growth in Christ, the lens cracks.

Remember the prodigal son? He left home with his inheritance and began living like a playboy. For a while, it was great. Friends gathered around. Cute chicks to be with. Wild nights. Big spending. Slowly, he changed—his countenance altered. If somebody could have taken snapshots, it would have shown up. We would be able to look into his face and see something different—something dreadfully wrong.

One day the money ran out. So did the parties, the "friends," and the pretty girls. The young prodigal desperately needed a job to keep himself alive. He got one. Just over the ridge and outside of town, a pig farmer hired him for considerably less than minimum wage. His job was slopping the hogs. Some days he bent down and ate out of the trough with them because he had no food and no money. Many nights he crawled through the mud, up into the pigpen, and slept with them because he had nowhere to go to stay warm. No picture was ever taken; it would have broken the camera.

The prodigal had gotten uglier and uglier on the inside, until finally it showed up on the outside. His ugly heart-attitude and ugly lifestyle turned into ugly circumstances. Pros can't make that look pretty, no matter how much they retouch their portraits.

What kind of things can alter your youthful good looks? What unattractive traits threaten to crack the viewfinder of God's camera?

Impurity. Whenever young people get involved in deep sexual relationships, something filters through onto their faces. I can't quite put my finger on it, but it's a certain hard look. One that says, "I'm toughened by experiencing things before my time, from dallying with things no one my age should." I've known girls who gave themselves away in cheap, meaningless sex. Innocence crept out of their faces, and ruggedness replaced it.

Resentment. This is kin to anger and rebellion. As this bitter emotion rears its ugly head, teenagers who let it take them over experience a slow change that comes into their countenances. You have probably seen it in classmates. It's an angry look. An expression that says, "I want to get even—I've been hurt, and I want to get even." The stronger the resentment grows, the clearer the mean stare comes into focus. A slight crack starts its way across the camera lens.

Selfishness. The I-me-my-mine-myself philosophy grips many young people. With a monster face, it begins transforming its victims. From the hairline to the chin and between the cheeks a strange look develops—one of jealousy or envy or greed. As it swells within, it glows without. When it does, put your cameras away.

There are also things that radiate beauty. For a beauty-conscious world like ours, I would think such a hope would perk up ears. True beauty, if that's what you're after, comes from the inside. It, too, can be captured in photographs. It begins with sincere devotion, yieldedness to God's Spirit, and closeness to Christ. No hype, I promise, and it has nothing to do with the cheap looks the world is after.

Now, hold still. *Click!* Got your picture. I wonder what we will see after the picture develops?

In His Image:

> When Moses came down from Mount Sinai with two tablets of the Testimony in his hands, he was not aware that his face was radiant because he had spoken with the Lord (Exod. 34:29).

Check for camera cracks:

1. Look at snapshots of yourself from the past two years. See any changes in your countenance?
2. Secretly look into the faces of classmates who you know for a fact have allowed camera-breaking traits to take them over. Can you see it in their faces?
3. Do a study of the word *countenance* in the Bible.

28

When You Can't Cope

Dave and Tim were good friends. They also had similar problems at home—constant fighting with parents—besides trouble at school. Both were juniors. Drugs played a big part in their downfall. I guess they thought they needed something to make them feel better. It didn't work. When they came down off a high the problems got worse. So they got high more often.

When that habit grew into harder drugs, they both changed completely. The arguments at home intensified. One night Dave busted his dad in the mouth and stormed out of the house. Upon calling his friend, the two decided to run away from home. With no money and nowhere to go, they set out.

Then Tim had a brilliant idea. They could go to a nearby car lot, break into a couple of the cars, rip off some stereos, and sell them "hot" to make a few bucks. That would at least help them get by until they could figure out what to do.

It was a piece of cake. Dave and Tim just knocked out a window, climbed in, unwired the stereo, and went to the next car. With four cassette decks in hand, they were surrounded by police cars from out of the night! Officers had been watching them all along. Before they could move, both were spread-eagled over a car hood . . . frisked . . . handcuffed . . . and stuffed into a squad car. Frightened, they confessed the whole plot.

Heartbroken parents posted bail for the boys. Big questions were raised about whether they would be treated as juveniles or adults. The car dealer wanted them jailed, since they had committed a felony crime and had caused more than one thousand dollars worth of damages. It seemed like the last straw for two guys who had grown totally unable to cope. They made a secret pact.

That warm summer night, after returning home, a very dejected Tim waited for the rest of the family to fall asleep. He flipped on his unplugged window fan. It didn't go, so he picked up the cord and got an idea. Dropping the cord, he sneaked into the bathroom. He took out a plastic bucket and filled it three-fourths full of water. He carried it back into his room, putting it down on the floor beneath the window fan. Then he put one foot into the bucket. Picking up the cord, seventeen-year-old Tim laid his index finger alongside one of the plug prongs. With no apparent hope in sight, he stuck the plug into the electricity socket while still holding his finger against the prong.

When Tim didn't come down the next morning, his mother came to find him. Tim was lying back across his bed. He looked asleep. Suddenly, his mother caught a glimpse of his foot in the bucket. She walked over to touch him. He felt cold . . . clammy . . . slightly hard. Quickly, she put a hand against his face. Tim was dead. Suicide.

Less than a mile away, Dave was carrying out his end of the pact. With two sharp strokes of one thin razor blade, his wrists were slashed. The sight of gushing blood and the immediate pain caused him to pass out. Fifteen minutes seemed like a long time for Dave to be in the bathroom. His dad called him. No answer. Ten more minutes passed. Dad pounded on the bathroom door. No answer. It was locked! He put a shoulder to the door a couple of times and knocked it in. Dave was on the floor—blood everywhere! Paramedics arrived just in time. Dave is in a psychiatric ward. He promises to finalize his agreement with Tim. One wonders if Dave will ever recover . . . if he will ever be able to cope with all that has happened . . . if he will have enough hope to begin his life again.

The aspects of this story are showing up more and more in teenage trauma cases: intense troubles, inability to cope, drugs, greater intensity until the lid blows, running away from home, lawbreaking, and suicide. Whenever the devil gains complete control of a life—and distorts the self-image of a person, making him or her feel empty and beyond worth—serious consequences are on the march. These symptoms should not be ignored!

If you are being drowned in a tidal wave of relentless troubles—stop! Get some help! Don't do anything foolish! Satan is concentrating his attack upon you and aims to destroy you. Please, don't laugh it off. You—the wonderful, precious, vibrant you—are being robbed of the image God created in you. That image is his own. Turn to him before it's too late.

Oh, by the way, the story of Dave and Tim is true. Very sadly true.

In His Image:

> He [God] will not let your foot slip—he who watches over you will not slumber. . . . the Lord is your shade at your right hand (Ps. 121:3, 5).

Find help to cope.

1. Find a verse in the Book of Psalms to memorize, one that brings you hope and peace and comfort. Claim it for those tough days.
2. Confide in an adult you trust. Tell him or her your deep fears, hurts, or need for help.
3. Think about the story of Dave and Tim. Do you know anyone who has committed suicide? Is that person's story similar?

29

The Struggles of String Cutting

You don't have to tell me that you're wanting to break free from your parents. You want to be your own person. You want individuality. Independence. Freedom to make more of your own choices. You want to do it *your* way. For years your parents have been saying, "Clean up your room," "Comb your hair," "Don't wear that," "Take a shower," "Improve your grades," "Go to church," "Choose nice friends," and "Do your homework." You really do love your parents, but you are getting a little tired of hearing all that.

No problem. That's normal. Yeah, you heard me right—*normal*! a growing desire for independence is part of maturing and becoming self-reliant. It's the old robin-climbing-out-of-the-nest scene. Just remember that earning your wings might include a few crash landings.

I'll tell you what is *not* normal. Screaming your angry disgust at the top of your lungs is not normal. Neither is slamming doors nor pouting. The same goes for "the silent treatment." Turning your stereo up to decibels unbearable to neighboring cities doesn't make it. Nor does refusing to eat. Storming out of the house in a huff is not a smart way to show your independence. Equally dumb is lashing out at someone who is innocent, such as a brother or sister. And, of course, there is the ever-popular tactic of making threats (especially running away from home). Uncool.

Oh, the struggles of string cutting! This is one of the hardest stages of becoming the whole you. But let's face it. The day is fast approaching when you will be on your own. Sooner than you think! And believe it or not, you will look back and it will seem as if the whole phase lasted only a moment. How terrific it will be if you don't have to look back upon these days with sorrowful regret.

May I share another secret? Independence isn't always as fantastic as you might think. Sometimes it's lonely. Scary. You know, being young has advantages, too. Like being care-free and blind to huge worries, being free to laugh and play without responsibilities and a time schedule, being able to be satisfied with the smallest and simplest of things.

Some people make the great mistake of thinking that freedom means being accountable only to self. What rude awakenings they find on the morning pillow of their identity crisis! There is no such "freedom" in this rat-race world. What we have been duped into calling freedom is only selfishness, which causes the worst kind of slavery. True freedom comes from growing strong in Jesus Christ.

Responsibility can be a hard row to hoe some days. The burdens will feel twice as heavy as your own weight. What you hoped would be the end of the work turns out to be the beginning of more. The choices get mixed up and unclear. Decisions on the spur of the moment will no longer be as simple as they were as a teenager. Hey! I'm not trying to spook you; I'm just letting you peek through the keyhole of truth.

You see, more freedom always means greater responsibility. You may have been led to believe that more freedom means fewer hassles. Wrong. Oh, sure, the hassles with your parents will gradually diminish. However, new people will jump up to take their place. People like your college dorm supervisor, your boss, your fiancé(e), your apartment-building neighbors, the electric company, the insurance agent, the nice store that gave you a credit card, and the mechanic who fixed your car, which still won't run.

Exciting, huh? Bet you can't wait to get out there on your own, earning six dollars less than the amount of your bills each month. Getting a whole quarter-an-hour raise every year, whether you deserve it or not. Paying your own taxes. Changing your own flat tires. Buying your own groceries and cooking your own meals. That's freedom. Ready for a big piece?

What's that you said? Not yet? I don't blame you. This period of your life is designed by God for self-awareness, not self-sufficiency. Think about this before you take the scissors to your mother's apron strings.

In His Image:

. . . Jesus said "If you hold to my teaching, you are really my disciples. Then you will know the truth, and the truth will set you free. . . . So if the Son sets you free, you will be free indeed" (John 8:31–32, 36).

You're Worth It!

Dare to cut an apron string and become independent enough to do one of these on your own:

1. Talk to your parents and find out what it was like when they were young and on their own for the very first time.

2. Think about these questions and come up with some answers: What are the consequences of irresponsibility? Of hanging onto the apron strings when it's time to let go and grow up? Of rushing out too soon?
3. Give a testimony at a youth activity about how the Lord is helping you prepare for the day of your independence.

30

Becoming Extra-Special

These questions all have something in common—they can be answered with the same two words. Can you figure out the answer?

What can help you really feel good about yourself?
What can give you a sense of being "somebody"?
What does every person long for in the soul?
What makes a person work harder at his or her job?
What does every would-be romantic hope for?
What makes a dog wag its tail and come running?
What makes a stray cat finally become the family pet?
What pleases God as he reaches out to man?
What motivates a teacher to stick with it?
Why does a hospital volunteer do that stuff for free?
What makes a friend a friend?

Being needed—that's it! We all need to feel needed by others, to believe that we bring them something special. That we offer as a person a unique joy unavailable anywhere else. That we can complete the world of others a bit better, because we are who we are. And no one else can be that.

Nearly everything that lives wants to be needed. Have you ever seen "A Charlie Brown Christmas"? When Charlie and Linus go to find a Christmas tree for the group's nativity play, a small scrawny one is chosen. The needles are falling out. It's about two feet tall. Linus balks at buying such an ugly tree, but Charlie Brown says, "No, we must get this tree! It *needs* us." Can that be? That a Christmas tree *needs* a home? You tell me. My kids say it's so.

Isolation. Not being needed. Becoming an island. These are the things that kill a person down inside. We all wish to be extra-special to someone in some way. Being all alone is a painful existence.

Yesterday I talked with a young woman. She is in her twenties. Her physical appearance is not very dynamic, although she tries hard to belong. I watched her cry streams of tears over being single and not having had many dates. Her dream is to become a wife and mother. Hope is nearly gone. What she would do if only someone needed her! With so much to give and so eager to give it, the misery is tightened when she comes home to an empty house every night.

She said to me, as I listened with heartfelt concern, "Do you know what it is like to eat alone not one or two days, but every day? Do you know what it is like to watch television alone? Or to listen to the stereo alone? Or to go for a walk alone? I like to play Scrabble, but who is there to play with? I'm tired of playing solitaire!"

This is the last chapter. I wish I could somehow draw this all to a perfect conclusion, but with such an individual, personal subject as this, there is no way. Still, it *will* all come together for you as you keep contact with heaven. That is the way it must be. For we're all different pieces of clay, which must be spun upon the Master Potter's wheel to reach that perfect design he has in mind for each of us. Chew on what you have read in these chapters, and the picture will gradually come into focus.

Then you will be ready. "Ready for what?" you ask. Ready to give yourself away. Isn't that strange? Once you grow strong in self-worth, you need to give of yourself. You will crave it, because it brings satisfaction.

Wow! This stuff is almost philosophical. It makes my head spin! Nonetheless, I know what a rewarding, special feeling I have about God and myself in my heart, when I have the privilege of pouring my life into the lives of others. Being needed in this world is what God uses to form us into our best selves.

You become extra-special when you share yourself—the beautiful creation God made you to be—with other people. When they sense your warmth and compassion and tenderness. When they can laugh or weep with you. When they can come to you for comfort. Yes, then you become your best.

Vulnerable? You bet you are. And you will get hurt. But you will recover—because you are God's child, and he is stamping his image on your life. That's what really matters to you. You want to model God's truth—so that all people can become the persons they were meant to be.

I can't resist one last tidbit of advice. Be authentic. Don't put chrome all over yourself. Or wax. Or plastic. Don't be fake. Synthetic people have not found true worth. Baloney people aren't free to be real, because the real person within them has never been set free by God's grace. They remain doves in a cage, never knowing or experiencing the joy of having something genuine to give—themselves.

This crazy, upside-down world of ours needs you. You may be young, but your hour is coming. And the world *needs* you to shine when that hour arrives. So bravely become comfortable with yourself. That will take some doing.

But you *are* worth it!

In His Image:

The Lord will fulfill his purpose for me; your love, O Lord, endures forever—do not abandon the work of your hands" (Ps. 138:8).

You're Worth It!

One of these needs you:

1. Go to your area's nursing home with a friend or two and visit with a few of the lonely people. They need you.
2. Encourage someone today, but not just anyone. Carefully choose the one who needs you from out of the crowd.
3. Read this book again.